美国原版经典语文课本

美国语文

THE ECLECTIC READERS

（英汉双语全译版）

3

WILLIAM H. MCGUFFEY

〔美〕威廉·H·麦加菲/编　邱　宏　周　婕/译

天津社会科学院出版社

U0582137

图书在版编目（CIP）数据

美国语文：英汉双语全译版. 3 /（美）麦加菲著；邱宏，周婕译.
—天津：天津社会科学院出版社，2012.1
（美国原版经典语文课本 / 刘津主编）

ISBN 978-7-80688-745-5

Ⅰ. ①美⋯　Ⅱ. ①麦⋯ ②邱⋯ ③周⋯　Ⅲ. ①英语课—小学—
美国—教材　Ⅳ. ① G624.311

中国版本图书馆 CIP 数据核字（2011）第 271473 号

出 版 发 行：天津社会科学院出版社
出　版　人：项　新
地　　　址：天津市南开区迎水道 7 号
邮　　　编：300191
电话 / 传真：（022）23366354
　　　　　　（022）23075303
电 子 信 箱：tssap@public.tpt.tj.cn
印　　　刷：北京金秋豪印刷有限公司

开　　　本：710×1000 毫米　1/16
印　　　张：16
字　　　数：400 千字
版　　　次：2012 年 1 月第 1 版　2014 年 8 月第 2 次印刷
定　　　价：39.80 元

版权所有　翻印必究

CONTENTS

LESSON 1
THE SHEPHERD BOY

◆

牧 童

either   *trickle*   *fancied*   *murmur*   *reflected*

glossy   *entered*   *shepherd*   *chestnuts*   *command*

1. Little Roy led his sheep down to pasture,
   And his cows, by the side of the brook;
But his cows never drank any water,
   And his sheep never needed a crook.

2. For the pasture was gay as a garden,
   And it glowed with a flowery red;
But the meadows had never a grass blade,
   And the brooklet—it slept in its bed:

3. And it lay without sparkle or murmur,
      Nor reflected the blue of the skies;
   But the music was made by the shepherd,
      And the sparkle was all in his eyes.

4. Oh, he sang like a bird in the summer!
      And, if sometimes you fancied a bleat,
   That, too, was the voice of the shepherd,
      And not of the lambs at his feet.

5. And the glossy brown cows were so gentle
      That they moved at the touch of his hand
   O'er the wonderful, rosy-red meadow,
      And they stood at the word of command.

6. So he led all his sheep to the pasture,
      And his cows, by the side of the brook;
   Though it rained, yet the rain never pattered
      O'er the beautiful way that they took.

7. And it wasn't in Fairyland either,
      But a house in the midst of the town,
   Where Roy, as he looked from the window,
      Saw the silvery drops trickle down.

8. For his pasture was only a table,
      With its cover so flowery fair,
   And his brooklet was just a green ribbon,
      That his sister had lost from her hair.

9. And his cows were but glossy horse-chestnuts,
      That had grown on his grandfather's tree;
   And his sheep only snowy-white pebbles,
      He had brought from the shore of the sea.

10. And at length when the shepherd was weary,
    And had taken his milk and his bread,
    And his mother had kissed him and tucked him,
    And had bid him "good night" in his bed;

11. Then there entered his big brother Walter,
    While the shepherd was soundly asleep,
    And he cut up the cows into baskets,
    And to jackstones turned all of the sheep.

(Emily S. Oakey)

【中文阅读】

1. 小罗伊赶着兰群来到牧场，
   将牛群驱赶到小溪边；
   牛群不需在溪边喝水，
   羊群也不需他挥舞牧鞭。

2. 牧场像花园一样绚丽多彩
   散发着亮丽的红色光芒。
   可这片土地却寸草不生，
   小溪也只在自己的温床上静静流淌。

3. 它既不闪闪发光，也不喃喃低语，
   更不会折射出晴空的湛蓝；
   小牧童哼起欢快的歌谣，
   眼中闪烁着迷人的光芒。

4. 哇，他就像夏日的小鸟在快唱！
   假如你恍若听到咩咩的声音，
   那一定是牧童在欢唱，
   而非他脚边的小羊羔。

5. 油亮闪亮的棕色母牛多么温顺，
   在牧童的轻抚下，
   牛群漫步在玫瑰红的欢乐草地上，
   主人一声令下便让它们停下。

6. 他就这样领着牛羊，
   在小溪边游荡；
   尽管天开始下雨，
   可雨滴并不似往日美丽的模样啪嗒啪嗒洒落下来。

7. 这里并不是什么仙境乐园，
   只不过是镇上一处屋舍，
   罗伊从这里还能看到
   窗外倾泻而下的闪光雨滴。

8. 他的牧场也不过是一张桌子，
   上面铺满各色花瓣；
   那潺潺小溪
   只是妹妹头上掉落的一条绿色丝带。

9. 温顺的牛群
   是从祖父种植的七叶树上采来的光滑叶片；
   可爱的羊群
   也不过是用海边拣的雪白鹅卵石来充当。

10. 牧童终于厌倦了这个游戏，
    喝光牛奶、吃完面包之后，
    妈妈令他上床睡觉，亲吻了他，
    轻轻道声"晚安"。

11. 就在牧童酣睡之际，
    大哥沃尔特走了进来，
    他将撕碎的牛群扔进篮子，
    用小石子取代了罗伊的羊群。

（爱米莉·奥凯）

4

LESSON 2
JOHNNY'S FIRST SNOWSTORM

◆

乔尼初次见雪

country   *groves*   *iosing*   *sugar*   *freezes*

1. Johnny Reed was a little boy who never had seen a snowstorm till he was six years old. Before this, he had lived in a warm country, where the sun shines down on beautiful orange groves, and fields always sweet with flowers.

2. But now he had come to visit his grandmother, who lived where the snow falls in winter. Johnny was standing at the window when the snow came down.

3. "O mamma!" he cried, joyfully, "do come quick, and see these little

white birds flying down from heaven."

4. "They are not birds, Johnny," said mamma, smiling.

5. "Then maybe the little angels are losing their feathers! Oh! do tell me what it is; is it sugar? Let me taste it," said Johnny. But when he tasted it, he gave a little jump—it was so cold.

6. "That is only snow, Johnny," said his mother.

7. "What is snow, mother?"

8. "The snowflakes, Johnny, are little drops of water that fall from the clouds. But the air through which they pass is so cold it freezes them, and they come down turned into snow."

9. As she said this, she brought out an old black hat from the closet. "See, Johnny! I have caught a snowflake on this hat. Look quick through this glass, and you will see how beautiful it is."

10. Johnny looked through the glass. There lay the pure, feathery snowflake like a lovely little star.

11. "Twinkle, twinkle, little star!" he cried in delight. "Oh! please show me more snow-flakes, mother."

12. So his mother caught several more, and they were all beautiful.

13. The next day Johnny had a fine play in the snow, and when he came in, he said, "I love snow; and I think snowballs are a great deal prettier than oranges."

【中文阅读】

1. 乔尼·瑞德是个小男孩，直到六岁，他才看到暴风雪。此前，他一直生活在地球的暖热带地区。在那里，阳光洒满大片美丽的橘树林，田野里到处都是芬芳扑鼻的鲜花。

2. 但是，现在他要去看望奶奶，那里的冬天常会下雪。每当雪花纷飞的时候，乔尼就会站在窗前定睛观望。

3. 他高兴地大喊："妈妈，快过来，瞧，这些白色的小鸟从天堂飞下来了。"

4. 妈妈笑着对他说："乔尼，那不是小鸟。"

5. "那么，可能是小天使掉落的羽毛吧！哦，快告诉我，那是什么，是糖吗？我想尝一下。"乔尼说。但是，就在品尝雪花时，他不禁惊跳起来——太凉了。

6. 妈妈说："那不过是雪而已，乔尼。"

7. "妈妈，雪是什么？"

8. "乔尼，雪就是从云彩上掉落的小水滴。但是，水滴从天上掉下来时，寒冷的空气将它们凝结住了，所以变成了从天而降的雪花。"

9. 她一边说着，一边从壁橱里取出一顶黑色的旧帽子。"看，乔尼！我用帽子接住了一片雪花。透过这块玻璃，你就知道雪花有多么美了。"

10. 乔尼透过玻璃看着雪花，那片纯净轻柔的雪花就像一颗可爱的小星星。

11. "哇，小星星还一闪一闪的呢！妈妈，再让我多看点雪花吧！"乔尼欢呼起来。

12. 于是，妈妈又抓住了一些雪花，都是那么漂亮！

13. 第二天，乔尼在雪地里开心地玩耍，从外面回家后，他说："我太喜欢雪了，雪球可比橘子好玩多了。"

LESSON 3
LET IT RAIN

◇

下雨吧

daughter   quench   wreaths   butter   thirsty

1. *Rose.* See how it rains! Oh dear, dear, dear! how dull it is! Must I stay in doors all day?

2. *Father.* Why, Rose, are you sorry that you had any bread and butter for breakfast, this morning?

3. *Rose.* Why, father, what a question! I should be sorry, indeed, if I could not get any.

4. *Father.* Are you sorry, my daughter, when you see the flowers and the trees growing in the garden?

5. *Rose.* Sorry? No, indeed. Just now, I wished very much to go out and see them,—they look so pretty.

6. *Father.* Well, are you sorry when you see the horses, cows, or sheep drinking at the brook to quench their thirst?

7. *Rose.* Why, father, you must think I am a cruel girl, to wish that the poor horses that work so hard, the beautiful cows that give so much nice milk, and the pretty lambs should always be thirsty.

8. *Father.* Do you not think they would die, if they had no water to drink?

9. *Rose.* Yes, sir, I am sure they would. How shocking to think of such a thing!

10. *Father.* I thought little Rose was sorry it rained. Do you think the trees and flowers would grow, if they never had any water on them?

11. *Rose.* No, indeed, father, they would be dried up by the sun. Then

we should not have any pretty flowers to look at, and to make wreaths of for mother.

12. *Father.* I thought you were sorry it rained. Rose, what is our bread made of?

13. *Rose.* It is made of flour, and the flour is made from wheat, which is ground in the mill.

14. *Father.* Yes, Rose, and it was rain that helped to make the wheat grow, and it was water that turned the mill to grind the wheat. I thought little Rose was sorry it rained.

15. *Rose.* I did not think of all these things, father. I am truly very glad to see the rain falling.

【中文阅读】

1. 罗斯：瞧，又下雨了！唉，天哪，天哪，天哪！多么无聊呀！难道我一整天都要待在家里？

2. 爸爸：罗斯，今天的早餐多么丰盛呀，有面包和奶油。你为什么不高兴呢？

3. 罗斯：为什么，爸爸，您怎么这样问呀！如果我没事可干，的确不高兴呀。

4. 爸爸：亲爱的女儿，当你看到花园里盛开的鲜花和茂密的树木时，也会不高兴吗？

5. 罗斯：不高兴？应该不会吧。刚才，我只是希望能出去看看它们——它们实在太美了。

6. 爸爸：好吧，当你看到小牛、小羊、小马在溪边饮水解渴时，也会不高兴吗？

7. 罗斯：为什么，爸爸，您一定认为我是一个冷酷无情的小女孩，总希望那些可怜的小马不知疲惫地工作，希望那些漂亮的小牛只会产奶，希望那些可爱的小羊总会口渴。

8. 爸爸：它们若没有水喝就会死掉，难道你不这样认为吗？

9. 罗斯：是的，现在，我也是这么想的。一想到这些事，多么可怕呀！

10. 爸爸：我以为小罗斯因为下雨而不高兴了。如果没有水滴落到它们身上，树木花草还会长大吗？这些你想过没有？

11. 罗斯：它们不会长大了，爸爸。它们会被太阳烤干的。那么，我们也就看不到美丽的鲜花，不能给妈妈编织花环了。

12. 爸爸：我以为你会因为下雨而伤心呢。罗斯，我们吃的面包是由什么做成的？

13. 罗斯：是由面粉做的，面粉是由麦子通过磨而制成的。

14. 爸爸：是的，罗斯，正是雨水促使小麦成熟，也正是水使磨盘碾碎了麦子。我还以为小罗斯不喜欢下雨呢。

15. 罗斯：爸爸，我没有想过这么多事情。我真的很高兴看到下雨了。

LESSON 4
CASTLE-BUILDING

◇

建造城堡

anger	castle	foundation	rattling	tower
dismay	sofa	interested	passion	pile
mimic	nodded	exclaimed	already	spilled

1. "O pussy!" cried Herbert, in a voice of anger and dismay, as the blockhouse he was building fell in sudden ruin. The playful cat had rubbed against his mimic castle, and tower and wall went rattling down upon the floor.

2. Herbert took up one of the blocks and threw it fiercely at pussy. Happily, it passed over her and did no harm. His hand was reaching for

another block, when his little sister Hetty sprang toward the cat, and caught her up.

3. "No, no, no!" said she, "you sha'n't hurt pussy! She didn't mean to do it!"

4. Herbert's passion was over quickly, and, sitting down upon the floor, he covered his face with his hands, and began to cry.

5. "What a baby!" said Joe, his elder brother, who was reading on the sofa. "Crying over spilled milk does no good. Build it up again."

6. "No, I won't," said Herbert, and he went on crying.

7. "What's all the trouble here?" exclaimed papa, as he opened the door and came in.

8. "Pussy just rubbed against Herbert's castle, and it fell down," answered Hetty. "But she didn't mean to do it; she didn't know it would fall, did she, papa?"

9. "Why, no! And is that all the trouble?"

10. "Herbert!" his papa called, and held out his hands. "Come." The little boy got up from the floor, and came slowly, his eyes full of tears, and stood by his father.

11. "There is a better way than this, my boy," said papa. "If you had taken that way, your heart would have been light already. I should have heard you singing over your blocks instead of crying. Shall I show you that way?"

12. Herbert nodded his head, and papa sat down on the floor by the pile of blocks, with his little son by his side, and began to lay the foundation for a new castle.

【中文阅读】

1. 赫伯特正在建造的城堡突然倒塌了，他带着愤怒和沮丧叫喊道："哇，可恶的小猫！"调皮的小猫咪恰巧从他的模型城堡边窜过去。

2. 赫伯特拿起一块积木，拼命地扔向那只小猫。积木从它身边擦肩而过，但并没有伤到他。他又去拿另一块积木，这时，小妹妹海蒂跑过来，抱起了小猫咪。

3. "不，不要，别这样！"她说，"你不能伤害小猫咪！它不是有意的！"

4. 赫伯特顿时怒火中烧，坐在地板上，双手捂住小脸哭了起来。

5. 正坐在沙发上看书的哥哥乔开腔了："真是个小孩子！哭也没用呀，再建一次就行了。"

6. 赫伯特一边哭着，一边说："我才不干呢。"

7. 爸爸开门走进来，问道："这旦发生什么事了？"

8. 海蒂抢先回答："小猫咪从赫伯特建造的城堡边经过，把它弄垮了。但是，它也不是有意的。它根本不知道城堡会倒掉，是吗，爸爸？"

9. "当然不知道了！这就是你们的麻烦？"

10. 爸爸一边伸出双手，一边说："赫伯特，过来。"小男孩从地板上起来，慢慢走过去，眼里噙着泪水，站在爸爸身边。

11. 爸爸说："我的孩子，还有一个好办法解决这个问题，如果你能照做的话，心里就会好受些。我应该听到你为积木歌唱，而不是为它哭泣。让我来教你吗？"

12. 赫伯特点了点头，爸爸坐在积木旁边的地板上，小儿子依偎在他身边，开始为一座新城堡奠基。

LESSON 5

CASTLE-BUILDING(CONCLUDED)

◇

建造城堡（结束篇）

string	paper	eagerly	dashed	case
crash	dishes	retorted	sentence	tray

1. Soon, Herbert was as much interested in castle-building as he had been a little while before. He began to sing over his work. All his trouble was gone.

2. "This is a great deal better than crying, isn't it?" said papa.

3. "Crying for what?" asked Herbert, forgetting his grief of a few minutes before.

4. "Because pussy knocked your castle over."

5. "Oh!" A shadow flitted across his face, but was gone in a moment, and he went on building as eagerly as ever.

6. "I told him not to cry over spilled milk," said Joe, looking down from his place on the sofa.

7. "I wonder if you didn't cry when your kite string broke," retorted Herbert.

8. "Losing a kite is quite another thing," answered Joe, a little dashed. "The kite was gone forever; but your blocks were as good as before, and you had only to build again."

9. "I don't see," said papa, "that crying was of any more use in your case then in Herbert's. Sticks and paper are easily found, and you had only to go to work and make another kite." Joe looked down at his book, and went on reading. By this time the castle was finished.

10. "It is ever so much nicer than the one pussy knocked down," said

Hetty. And so thought Herbert, as he looked at it proudly from all sides.

11. "If pussy knocks that down, I'll—"

12. "Build it up again," said papa, finishing the sentence for his little boy.

13. "But, papa, pussy must not knock my castles down. I can't have it," spoke out Herbert, knitting his forehead.

14. "You must watch her, then. Little boys, as well as grown up people, have to be often on their guard. If you go into the street, you have to look out for the carriages, so as not to be run over, and you have to keep out of people's way.

15. "In the house, if you go about heedlessly, you will be very apt to run against some one. I have seen a careless child dash suddenly into a room just as a servant was leaving it with a tray of dishes in her hands. A crash followed."

16. "It was I, wasn't it?" said Hetty.

17. "Yes, I believe it was, and I hope it will never happen again."

18. Papa now left the room, saying, "I don't want any more of this crying over spilled milk, as Joe says. If your castles get knocked down, build them up again."

【中文阅读】

1. 很快，赫伯特就对新建的城堡产生了更浓厚的兴趣，而且开始为自己的工作欢呼了。他所有的问题都解决了。

2. "这样可比无谓的哭泣好多了，难道不是吗？"爸爸说。

3. "为什么要哭呀？"赫伯特问道，他已经忘记了刚才的伤痛。

4. "因为小猫碰倒了你的城堡呀。"

5. "噢！"一丝阴影掠过他的面庞，但很快就消失了，他继续建筑自己的城堡。

6. "我告诉过他，别为已经出现的失败而沮丧。"乔一边说着，一边坐在沙发上向这边观望。

7. 赫伯特反驳道："我想知道，如果你的风筝线断了，你是否真的不哭。"

8. "风筝丢了就是另一回事了，"乔回答道，情绪有点激动。"风筝若没了，就永远也找不回来了。但是你的积木却完好如初，只需重新搭一座新的城堡就好了。"

9. 爸爸说："依我看，无论你，还是赫伯特，在这种情况下都不应该哭，一味地哭泣并没有用。棍棒和纸也很容易找到，你只要重新做一个风筝就好了。"乔低头看了看自己的书，不再出声了。这时，一座新的城堡已经建好了。

10. 海蒂说："它甚至比刚才那座被猫咪撞倒的城堡还好看。"赫伯特也这样认为，因为无论从哪一方面，他都为此感到骄傲。

11. "要是小猫再把它撞倒了，我就……"

12. "重新再搭一座。"爸爸赶紧接过了他的话茬。

13. "可是，爸爸，猫咪千万不能再把我的城堡撞倒了，我可受不了。"赫伯特皱着眉头，大喊道。

14. "那么，你自己要守护好它。无论小孩子，还是长大以后，都要做好自己的守护工作。如果你在大街上行走，一定要留心马车，不能被它撞倒，而且你还要留心别挡住其他人的路。"

15. "即使在房子里，如果你走路不小心，也会撞倒什么东西。我就曾经亲眼见过，在仆人举着一叠托盘离开时，一个粗心大意的小孩子猛然冲进屋里。不可避免地，盘子碎了一地。"

16. "这不正是我吗？"海蒂不好意思地说。

17. "是的，我也这么认为，希望以后再也不要发生同样的事情。"

18. "就像乔说得那样，我也不希望再听到为失败而哭泣的声音了。如果你的城堡倒掉了，再建一次就好了。"爸爸一边说着，一边离开了房间。

LESSON 6
LEND A HAND

———◇———

伸出一只手

tear   *daily*   *honor*   *tongues*   *suspicion*
envy   *forced*   *prompt*   *malicious*   *tomorrow*

1.

Lend a hand to one another
In the daily toil of life;
When we meet a weaker brother,
Let us help him in the strife.
There is none so rich but may,
In his turn, be forced to borrow;
And the poor man's lot to-day
May become our own to-morrow.

2.

Lend a hand to one another:
When malicious tongues have thrown
Dark suspicion on your brother,
Be not prompt to cast a stone.
There is none so good but may

Run adrift in shame and sorrow.
And the good man of to-day
May become the bad to-morrow.

3.

Send a hand to one another:
In the race for Honor's crown;
Should it fall upon your brother.
Let not envy tear it down.
Send a hand to all, we pray,
In their sunshine or their sorrow;
And the prize they've won to-day
May become our own to-morrow

LESSON 7
THE TRUANT

◆

逃 学

falsely   *attend*   *truant*   *conduct*   *therefore*
guilty   *haste*   *regular*   *struggled*   *ignorant*

1. James Brown was ten years old when his parents sent him to school. It was not far from his home, and therefore they sent him by himself.

2. But, instead of going to school, he was in the habit of playing truant. He would go into the fields, or spend his time with idle boys.

3. But this was not all. When he went home, he would falsely tell his mother that he had been to school, and had said his lessons very well.

4. One fine morning, his mother told James to make haste home from school, for she wished, after he had come back, to take him to his aunt's.

5. But, instead of minding her, he went off to the water, where there were some boats. There he met plenty of idle boys.

6. Some of these boys found that James had money, which his aunt had given him; and he was led by them to hire a boat, and to go with them upon the water.

7. Little did James think of the danger into which he was running. Soon the wind began to blow, and none of them knew how to manage the boat.

8. For some time, they struggled against the wind and the tide. At last, they became so tired that they could row no longer.

9. A large wave upset the boat, and they were all thrown into the water. Think of James Brown, the truant, at this time!

10. He was far from home, known by no one. His parents were ignorant of his danger. He was struggling in the water, on the point of being drowned.

11. Some men, however, saw the boys, and went out to them in a boat. They reached them just in time to save them from a watery grave.

12. They were taken into a house, where their clothes were dried. After a while, they were sent home to their parents.

13. James was very sorry for his conduct, and he was never known to be guilty of the same thing again.

14. He became regular at school, learned to attend to his books, and, above all, to obey his parents perfectly.

【中文阅读】

1. 詹姆斯·布朗十岁时，父母将他送到学校读书。学校离家并不太远，所以父母让他单独去上学。

2. 但是，他并没有按时去学校，反而玩起了逃学的游戏。他要么去田野里玩耍，要么就和游手好闲的孩子们一起消磨时光。

3. 情况并非如此简单。回到家后，他还欺骗父母，说自己去上学了，而且还说课程很精彩。

4. 一个晴空万里的早晨，妈妈告诉詹姆斯放学后早点回家，因为想带他一起去姨妈家玩。

5. 然而，他并没有将妈妈的嘱托放在心上，反而独自来到了海边，那里有很多很多的船。他还遇到了几个无所事事的小男孩。

6. 其中几个孩子发现詹姆斯身上带着钱，这可是姨妈以前给的零花钱；詹姆斯被他们诱导着去租一条小船，然后大家一起驶向大海。

7. 小詹姆斯根本没有意识到这次航行充满危险。很快，水面上刮起了大风，他们都不知道该如何控制小船。

8. 有那么一会儿，他们挣扎着逆风而行。后来，他们实在太累了，再也划不动船桨了。

9. 一个大浪打来，几个孩子全都落入水中。这时，再来看看詹姆斯·布朗——这个逃学的家伙！

10. 他已经离家很远了，而且没有人知道他去了哪里。爸爸妈妈根本不知道他已经陷入了危险之中。就在差点被淹死的危急关头，他奋力地在水中挣扎。

11. 然而，幸好有人看到他们了，并且乘船前来拯救他们。人们及时地救起了这些即将溺水而死的孩子。

12. 他们被带进了一所房子，将自己的湿衣服烤干。又过了一会儿，大家将孩子们纷纷送回了家。

13. 詹姆斯对自己的行为感到十分难过，从此，他再也没有为同样的事情而内疚过。

14. 他开始按时上学、认真听课了，更重要的是，他完全听任父母的安排，成了一个听话的好孩子。

LESSON 8
THE WHITE KITTEN
◇

小白猫

stroke　　*beggar*　　*streaks*　　*needful*　　*counsel*

1. My little white kitten's asleep on my knee;
   As white as the snow or the lilies is she;
   　　She wakes up with a pur
   　　When I stroke her soft fur:
   Was there ever another white kitten like her?

2. My little white kitten now wants to go out
   And frolic, with no one to watch her about;
   　　"Little kitten," I say,

"Just an hour you may stay,
And be careful in choosing your places to play."

3. But night has come down, when I hear a loud "mew;"
I open the door, and my kitten comes through;
    My white kitten! ah me!
    Can it really be she—
This ill-looking, beggar-like cat that I see?

4. What ugly, gray streaks on her side and her back!
Her nose, once as pink as a rosebud, is black!
    Oh, I very well know,
    Though she does not say so,
She has been where white kittens ought never to go.

5. If little good children intend to do right,
If little white kittens would keep themselves white,
    It is needful that they
    Should this counsel obey,
And be careful in choosing their places to play.

【中文阅读】

1. 小猫在我的膝盖上睡着了
   她身上的毛洁白如雪,
   像百合花一样纯洁;
   当我轻抚她的软发时,
   带着咕噜咕噜的声音她醒来了,
   其他小白猫能像她这样吗?

2. 我的小白猫现在要出去嬉闹,
   却没有人能守护她;

"小猫咪呀，"我说，
"你只能玩一个小时，
好好选个玩耍之地哟。"

3. 夜晚来临，我听到"喵喵"的叫声，
我打开门，小白猫进来了；
我的小白猫呀！哎呀呀！
这难道真的是她吗？
一只相貌丑陋、乞丐一样的小猫！

4. 背部和身上全是灰色条痕！
玫瑰花蕾般的粉红小鼻也染成了黑色！
哦，我好像明白了，
虽然她并没有说，
她肯定去了一个不该去的地方。

5. 如果小孩们能正确行事，
如果小白猫能保持洁白，
也就不必有这么多的规矩要遵守，
也要仔细选择玩耍的地方哟。

LESSON 9
THE BEAVER

海　狸

prefer	*trapper*	*forward*	*material*	*disturbing*
dumb	*chiefly*	*gnawing*	*America*	*cautiously*
height	*purpose*	*tighter*	*reminded*	*frequently*
obtain	*curious*	*inhuman*	*including*	*constructed*

1. The beaver is found chiefly in North America. It is about three and a half feet long, including the flat, paddle-shaped tail, which is a foot in length.

2. The long, shining hair on the back is chestnut-colored, while the fine, soft fur that lies next the skin, is grayish brown.

3. Beavers build themselves most curious huts to live in, and quite frequently a great number of these huts are placed close together, like the buildings in a town.

4. They always build their huts on the banks of rivers or lakes, for they swim much more easily than they walk, and prefer moving about in the water.

5. When they build on the bank of a running stream, they make a dam across the stream for the purpose of keeping the water at the height they wish.

6. These dams are made chiefly of mud, and stones, and the branches of trees. They are sometimes six or seven hundred feet in length, and are so constructed that they look more like the work of man than of little dumb beasts.

7. Their huts are made of the same material as the dams, and are round in shape. The walls are very thick, and the roofs are finished off with a thick layer of mud, sticks, and leaves.

8. They commence building their houses late in the summer, but do not get them finished before the early frosts. The freezing makes them tighter and stronger.

9. They obtain the wood for their dams and huts by gnawing through the branches of trees, and even through the trunks of small ones, with their sharp front teeth. They peel off the bark, and lay it up in store for winter food.

10. The fur of the beaver is highly prized. The men who hunt these animals are called trappers.

11. A gentleman once saw five young beavers playing. They would leap on the trunk of a tree that lay near a beaver dam, and would push one another off into the water.

12. He crept forward very cautiously, and was about to fire on the little creatures; but their amusing tricks reminded him so much of some little children he knew at home, that he thought it would be inhuman to kill them. So he left them without even disturbing their play.

【中文阅读】

1. 海狸主要出现在北美地区，包括如桨一样平坦的尾巴在内，身体总长约3.5英尺，仅它的尾巴就有一英尺长。

2. 它身后长长的光亮毛发是栗子色的，而紧靠皮肤的精美细柔皮毛则是略带浅灰的棕色。

3. 海狸为自己建造的居所大多奇形怪状，而且经常是大批海狸比邻而居，就像城市里的建筑物一样。

4. 它们总喜欢将自己的住所建造在河堤或湖边。因为它们在水中比在岸上行走更容易些，所以它们更喜欢在水中移动。

5. 当它们在潺潺的小溪边构建自己的巢穴时，往往会建造一条跨越溪流的大坝，目的是为了按照自己的意愿保证水流的高度。

6. 这些大坝主要是由泥土、石头和树枝构成。有时，它们建造的水坝足有六七百英尺长，如此完美的建筑，看起来更像是人类的杰作，绝非出自这些默不作声的小动物之手。

7. 它们的小屋和水坝都是由同样的材料建造而成，形状也都是圆形的。墙壁非常厚实，屋顶则由厚而稠的泥土、枝条和树叶组成。

8. 它们常常在夏末开始建造自己的小屋，但是并不会在冰冻初期结束这个工程。霜冻会使它们的房屋更加结实牢固。

9. 海狸用自己那尖而长的前牙不断地噬咬大树的细枝，它们甚至还会咬断小树的主干，从而为自己的小屋和水坝储存木材。它们会剥掉树皮，作为冬天的食物以备后用。

10. 海狸的皮毛极其珍贵。猎杀这类动物的人都被称做猎人。

11. 曾经有一位先生，亲眼看到过五只小海狸在玩耍。它们在自己建造的水坝附近嬉戏，大家都想跳过一根树干，于是彼此推搡着想让另外一个掉进水里。

12. 那位先生很谨慎地匍匐前进，随时准备袭击这些小生命；但是它们那有趣的把戏又使他想起了自己家中的小孩子，心里暗自寻思如此猎杀海狸是不人道的。于是，他悄悄地离开了，并没有打扰海狸们的嬉戏玩耍。

LESSON 10

THE YOUNG TEACHER

◇
——————— ◇ ———————

小老师

sign   *marks*   *parcels*   *venture*   *inquire*
chalk   *ruling*   *drawing*   *pictures*   *confused*

1. Charles Rose lived in the country with his father, who taught him to read and to write.

2. Mr. Rose told his son that, when his morning lessons were over, he might amuse himself for one hour as he pleased.

3. There was a river near by. On its bank stood the hut of a poor fisherman, who lived by selling fish.

4. His careful wife kept her wheel going early and late. They both

worked very hard to keep themselves above want.

5. But they were greatly troubled lest their only son should never learn to read and to write. They could not teach him themselves, and they were too poor to send him to school.

6. Charles called at the hut of this fisherman one day, to inquire about his dog, which was missing.

7. He found the little boy, whose name was Joe, sitting by the table, on which he was making marks with a piece of chalk. Charles asked him whether he was drawing pictures.

8. "No, I am trying to write," said little Joe, "but I know only two words. Those I saw upon a sign, and I am trying to write them."

9. "If I could only learn to read and write," said he, "I should be the happiest boy in the world."

10. "Then I will make you happy," said Charles. "I am only a little boy, but I can teach you that.

11. "My father gives me an hour every day for myself. Now, if you will try to learn, you shall soon know how to read and to write."

12. Both Joe and his mother were ready to fall on their knees to thank Charles. They told him it was what they wished above all things.

13. So, on the next day when the hour came, Charles put his book in his pocket, and went to teach Joe. Joe learned very fast, and Charles soon began to teach him how to write.

14. Some time after, a gentleman called on Mr. Rose, and asked him if he knew where Charles was. Mr. Rose said that he was taking a walk, he supposed.

15. "I am afraid," said the gentleman, "that he does not always amuse himself thus. I often see him go to the house of the fisherman. I fear he goes out in their boat."

16. Mr. Rose was much troubled. He had told Charles that he must never venture on the river, and he thought he could trust him.

17. The moment the gentleman left, Mr. Rose went in search of his son. He went to the river, and walked up and down, in hope of seeing the boat.

18. Not seeing it, he grew uneasy. He thought Charles must have gone a long way off. Unwilling to leave without learning something of him, he

went to the hut.

19. He put his head in at the window, which was open. There a pleasant sight met his eyes.

20. Charles was at the table, ruling a copybook Joe was reading to him, while his mother was spinning in the corner.

21. Charles was a little confused. He feared his father might not be pleased; but he had no need to be uneasy, for his father was delighted.

22. The next day, his father took him to town, and gave him books for himself and Joe, with writing paper, pens, and ink.

23. Charles was the happiest boy in the world when he came home. He ran to Joe, his hands filled with parcels, and his heart beating with joy.

【中文阅读】

1. 查尔斯·罗斯和父亲住在乡下。在那里，父亲教他读书和写字。

2. 罗斯先生告诉儿子，每天上午的课程结束后，他可以随意玩耍一个小时。

3. 他们的住处附近有一条河，河岸上有一个小屋，住着一个可怜的穷渔夫，靠打鱼为生。

4. 渔夫那勤劳的妻子总是从早忙到晚，一刻也不闲着。他们都很努力地想让自己的生活更好些。

5. 但是，他们又在为自己唯一的儿子无法学习而犯愁。他们既无法自己教孩子学习，又因为贫穷而没有能力送孩子去学校里学习。

6. 有一天，查尔斯来到这个渔夫家中，问他有没有看到一条走失的狗。

7. 他看到渔夫的儿子——一个名叫乔的小男孩正坐在桌子上，用一支粉笔在上面做记号。查尔斯问他是否在画画。

8. "没有，我在试着写字呢，"乔说，"但是，我只认识两个字，是从一个标牌上看到的，我正要试着写下来呢。"

9. "要是我能学习阅读和写字就好了，"他继续说，"那我就成了世界上最幸福的人。"

10. 查尔斯说："那么，我来让你幸福吧，我虽然只是一个小孩子，但是我能教你阅读和写字。"

11. "父亲每天都会给我一个小时的时间。如果你想学习，很快就能学会如何阅读、如何写字了。"

12. 乔和他的妈妈都快要跪下来感谢查尔斯了。他们告诉他，这正是自己最大的心愿。

13. 于是，在第二天可以自由活动的时候，查尔斯将书本放到口袋里，准备去给乔上课。乔非常聪明，学得很快，查尔斯已经开始教他如何写字了。

14. 过了一段时间，有一位绅士前来拜访罗斯先生，问他是否知道查尔斯在哪里。罗斯先生说，他以为查尔斯出去散步了。

15. 这位先生说："我很担心，他不会一直自己玩的。我经常看到他去渔夫住的小屋。我担心他会坐船出去。"

16. 罗斯先生有点慌乱了。他曾经嘱咐过查尔斯不要到河里去玩，那样很危险，而且他还以为应该相信孩子。

17. 就在那位先生离开后，罗斯也出去寻找儿子。他走到河边，来来回回地找，希望能看到小船。

18. 什么也没有看到，这让他更加心神不安了。他以为查尔斯已经离岸边很远了。他并不想如此一无所获地回家，于是便走向渔夫住的小屋。

19. 小屋有一扇打开的窗户，他探头进去观望，一幅令人愉快的画面映入他的眼帘。

20. 查尔斯正用笔在桌上的一本字帖上划着，乔在跟着他一起读，而乔的妈妈正在角落里纺纱。

21. 查尔斯有点困惑了。他害怕父亲不高兴，但他也不必为此感到不安，因为父亲看上去很快乐。

22. 第二天，父亲带他去城里，为他和乔分别买了课本，还有写字用的纸、笔和墨水。

23. 在回家的路上，查尔斯感到自己是最幸福的孩子。他两手拿着包裹，快速跑到乔的家中，高兴得心都快跳出来了。

LESSON 11

THE BLACKSMITH

◇

铁 匠

iron
eyelids
forge
intense

clinkerty
shrink
labor
hammer

1. Clink, clink, clinkerty clink!
   We begin to hammer at morning's blink,
      And hammer away
      Till the busy day,
   Like us, aweary, to rest shall sink.

2. Clink, clink, clinkerty clink!
   From labor and care we never will shrink;
      But our fires we'll blow
      Till our forges glow
   With light intense, while our eyelids wink.

3. Clink, clink, clinkerty clink!
   The chain we'll forge with many a link.
      We'll work each form

While the iron is warm,
With strokes as fast as we can think.

4. Clink, clink, clinkerty clink!
Our faces may be as black as ink,
    But our hearts are true
    As man ever knew,
And kindly of all we shall ever think.

【中文阅读】

1. 叮当，叮当，叮叮当！
当天空出现第一缕晨光，
我们开始敲打，不停劳作，
直到忙碌的太阳沉落，
疲倦地回去休息，和我们一样。

2. 叮当，叮当，叮叮当！
我们小心谨慎，不停地忙；
吹起熊熊火焰，
直到熔炉发烫，我们不停眨眼，
因那炉火炽热的强光。

3. 叮当，叮当，叮叮当！
一环一环锻成铁链长又长，
我们趁着烙铁热烫，
打造各种形状，
手起锤落，快如思想跳跃的闪光。

4. 叮当，叮当，叮叮当！
也许我们的脸黑得像墨水一样，
可是我们的心无比真挚，
正如人们一直所知，
我们也总是善待各方。

LESSON 12

A WALK IN THE GARDEN

◇

园中漫步

| shook | gravel | invited | assure | continued |
| plants | borders | enjoyed | meddle | admiring |

1. Frank was one day walking with his mother, when they came to a pretty garden. Frank looked in, and saw that it had clean gravel walks, and beds of beautiful flowers all in bloom.

2. He called to his mother, and said, "Mother, come and look at this pretty garden. I wish I might open the gate, and walk in."

3. The gardener, being near, heard what Frank said, and kindly invited

him and his mother to come into the garden.

4. Frank's mother thanked the man. Turning to her son, she said, "Frank, if I take you to walk in this garden, you must take care not to meddle with anything in it."

5. Frank walked along the neat gravel paths, and looked at everything, but touched nothing that he saw.

6. He did not tread on any of the borders, and was careful that his clothes should not brush the tops of the flowers, lest he might break them.

7. The gardener was much pleased with Frank, because he was so careful not to do mischief. He showed him the seeds, and told him the name of many of the flowers and plants.

8. While Frank was admiring the beauty of a flower, a boy came to the gate, and finding it locked, he shook it hard. But it would not open. Then he said, "Let me in; let me in; will you not let me in this garden?"

9. "No, indeed," said the gardener, "I will not let you in, I assure you; for when I let you in yesterday, you meddled with my flowers, and pulled some of my rare fruit. I do not choose to let a boy into my garden who meddles with the plants."

10. The boy looked ashamed, and when he found that the gardener would not let him in, he went slowly away.

11. Frank saw and felt how much happier a boy may be by not meddling with what does not belong to him.

12. He and his mother then continued their walk in the garden, and enjoyed the day very much. Before they left, the gardener gave each of them some pretty flowers.

【中文阅读】

1. 有一天，弗兰克和妈妈散步时看到了一个非常漂亮的花园。弗兰克忍不住探头向里观望，他看到一条铺满细碎卵石的洁净小路，花圃里到处都是盛开着的鲜花。

2. 他立刻呼唤妈妈："妈妈，快来看看这个美丽的花园。我真想打开门进去走

35

走。"

3. 正在附近的园丁听到了弗兰克的话，非常亲切地邀请他们进去。

4. 弗兰克的妈妈对园丁的好心表达了谢意，并回头对儿子说："弗兰克，如果我带你到花园里散步，你必须要小心，不能乱动任何花草树木。"

5. 弗兰克沿着洁净的碎石路小心地前行，他四处张望，小心翼翼地不敢碰触任何东西。

6. 他也没有踩踏任何超出道路边界的地方，很小心地不让自己的衣服刮蹭柔嫩的鲜花，唯恐折断它们。

7. 园丁对弗兰克的行为十分满意，因为他如此小心地不破坏任何花草。他带弗兰克认识了许多不同的种子，还告诉他诸多鲜花和植物的名称。

8. 正当弗兰克悠闲地欣赏着美丽的鲜花时，一个小男孩跑到门口来，他看到大门被锁，便使劲地摇晃着。但是，门却依然没有被打开。接着，他喊道："让我进去，让我进去，你不让我进这个花园了吗？"

9. 园丁对他说："是的，不让你进来了。我明确地告诉你，再也不许你进来了；因为昨天让你进来后，你把我的鲜花都弄坏了，不仅如此，还把那罕见的果实也摘了下来。我再也不允许一个随便破坏花草的小男孩进到花园里来了。"

10. 这个小男孩有点难为情，当他发现园丁再也不让自己进去之后，慢慢地走开了。

11. 不乱动本不属于自己的东西——做一个这样的好孩子多么快乐呀，弗兰克既看到也感受到了这一点。

12. 他和妈妈继续在花园里漫步，愉快地享受着这美好的一天。在离开之前，园丁分别给了母子俩一些美丽的鲜花。

LESSON 13

THE WOLF

◇

狼来了

wolf   *grieved*   *sleeve*   *neighbors*   *earnest*
axes   *clubs*   *order*   *single*   *destroy*

1. A boy was once taking care of some sheep, not far from a forest. Near by was a village, and he was told to call for help if there was any danger.

2. One day, in order to have some fun, he cried out, with all his might, "The wolf is coming! the wolf is coming!"

3. The men came running with clubs and axes to destroy the wolf. As they saw nothing they went home again, and left John laughing in his sleeve.

4. As he had had so much fun this time, John cried out again, the next

day, "The wolf! the wolf!"

5. The men came again, but not so many as the first time. Again they saw no trace of the wolf; so they shook their heads, and went back.

6. On the third day, the wolf came in earnest. John cried in dismay, "Help! help! the wolf! the wolf!" But not a single man came to help him.

7. The wolf broke into the flock, and killed a great many sheep. Among them was a beautiful lamb, which belonged to John.

8. Then he felt very sorry that he had deceived his friends and neighbors, and grieved over the loss of his pet lamb.

The truth itself is not believed,

From one who often has deceived.

【中文阅读】

1. 有一个小男孩曾经在离森林不远的地方牧羊。他住的村子就在附近，人们告诉他如果碰到了危险就赶紧大喊救命。

2. 有一天，他为了找点乐趣，使出吃奶的劲大喊道："狼来了！狼来了！"

3. 人们纷纷拿着棍棒和斧头跑来，准备对付大灰狼。然而他们并没有看到狼，于是就各自回家了，只留下约翰一个人捂袖偷笑。

4. 由于这次的行为让他感受到了诸多乐趣，于是，第二天约翰再次大喊："狼来了！狼来了！"

5. 人们再次赶来，但是已经不如上次那么多人了。结果，他们发现自己又上当了，根本没看到什么狼，人们只得各自摇着头回去了。

6. 到了第三天，狼真的来了。约翰惊慌失措地大喊道："救命！救命！狼真的来了！狼真的来了！"但是，这一次没有人前来帮他了。

7. 狼冲进了他的羊群，咬死了很多羊，而且，其中有一只温顺漂亮的小羊羔还是约翰的。

8. 终于，他为自己欺骗了朋友和邻居深感懊悔，也为失去了这么多可爱的羊而哀悼。

经常说谎的人，

即使说出了真理，也无人相信！

LESSON 14
THE LITTLE BIRD'S SONG

◇

小鸟之歌

melody   unnoticed   modest   content   Gracie

1. A little bird, with feathers brown,
      Sat singing on a tree;
   The song was very soft and low,
      But sweet as it could be.

2. The people who were passing by,
      Looked up to see the bird
   That made the sweetest melody
      That ever they had heard.

3. But all the bright eyes looked in vain;
      Birdie was very small,

And with his modest, dark-brown coat,
He made no show at all.

4. "Why, father," little Gracie said
"Where can the birdie be?
If I could sing a song like that,
I'd sit where folks could see."

5. "I hope my little girl will learn
A lesson from the bird,
And try to do what good she can,
Not to be seen or heard. "

6. "This birdie is content to sit
Unnoticed on the way,
And sweetly sing his Maker's praise
From dawn to close of day."

7. "So live, my child, all through your life,
That, be it short or long,
Though others may forget your looks,
They'll not forget your song."

【中文阅读】

1. 一只小鸟，长着棕色羽毛，
歇在枝头吟唱；
歌声温柔轻细，
可如此清脆悦耳。

2. 人们从树下路过，
仰头望视小鸟；

那美妙之音，
他们从未听见。

3. 众人明眼皆徒劳，
   鸟宝贝实在太小；
   身着朴实涤棕衣，
   一点让人看不见。

4. "哦，爸爸，"小格雷斯说，
   "鸟宝贝在哪呢？"
   "要是我像它那样唱得好听，
   我会坐得大家都能看见。"

5. "我期望我的乖女儿
   能从小鸟身上得到教训
   努力让自己做得更好，
   不求让人看见或听到。"

6. "小鸟知足地坐在
   不引人注目的地方，
   甜美地唱着造物主的颂歌，
   从黎明到日落。"

7. "我的孩子，生命本应如此度过，
   无论其短暂或久远，
   尽管他人会忘记你的容貌，
   但他们不会忘记你的歌声。"

LESSON 15

HARRY AND ANNIE

◇

哈利和安妮

least   *thaw*   *sliding*   *plunged*   *naturedly*
bade   *scatter*   *pretend*   *exploring*   *disobedient*

1. Harry and Annie lived a mile from town, but they went there to school every day. It was a pleasant walk down the lane, and through the meadow by the pond.

2. I hardly know whether they liked it better in summer or in winter. They used to pretend that they were travelers exploring a new country, and would scatter leaves on the road that they might find their way back again.

3. When the ice was thick and firm, they went across the pond. But their mother did not like to have them do this unless some one was with them.

4. "Don't go across the pond today, children," she said, as she kissed them and bade them good-by one morning; "it is beginning to thaw."

5. "All right, mother," said Harry, not very good-naturedly, for he was very fond of running and sliding on the ice. When they came to the pond, the ice looked hard and safe.

6. "There," said he to his sister, "I knew it hadn't thawed any. Mother is always afraid we shall be drowned. Come along, we will have a good time sliding. The school bell will not ring for an hour at least."

7. "But you promised mother," said Annie.

8. "No, I didn't. I only said 'All right,' and it is all right."

9. "I didn't say anything; so I can do as I like," said Annie.

10. So they stepped on the ice, and started to go across the pond. They had not gone far before the ice gave way, and they fell into the water.

11. A man who was at work near the shore, heard the screams of the children, and plunged into the water to save them. Harry managed to get to the shore without any help, but poor Annie was nearly drowned before the man could reach her.

12. Harry went home almost frozen, and told his mother how disobedient he had been. He remembered the lesson learned that day as long as he lived.

【中文阅读】

1. 哈利和安妮住在离市区一英里远的地方，但是他们每天都要去位于市区的学校上学。沿着小巷和牧场中的池塘边散步，是一件让人很愉快的事情。

2. 我不知道他们喜欢在鲜花盛开的夏季悠闲漫步，还是更喜欢在寒冷的冬季穿行。他们曾经假装自己是一个去新国度探险的旅行者，将路边的矮树丛纷纷拨开，以便于再次找到归途。

3. 当池塘里的水结成坚硬厚实的冰，他们就会直接在冰面上穿过。但是，妈妈却不想让他们这样，除非有人在旁随行。

4. 某天早上，在与孩子们吻别时，她说："孩子们，今天不要从冰面上直接穿越池塘了，因为冰已经开始融化了。"

5. "好吧，妈妈，"哈利有点不耐烦地回答，因为他非常喜欢在冰面上滑行。当他们来到池塘边时，冰面看上去还那么坚硬结实。

6. 他对妹妹说:"看,我就知道还没有融化呢。妈妈总是担心我们被淹死。来吧,我们再好好玩一次溜冰。学校的钟声至少还要一个小时才会响起来呢。"

7. 安妮说:"可是,你已经答应妈妈了。"

8. "不,我没有。我只是说'好',而且这也是'没关系的意思'。"

9. 安妮说:"我并没说什么,所以我可以做自己喜欢的事情。"

10. 于是,他们踏上了冰面,开始滑行着穿越池塘。还没走出多远,冰面就开始塌陷了,他俩都掉进了水中。

11. 一个正在岸边工作的人听到了孩子们的尖叫声,紧接着跳入水中救起了他们。哈利自己设法游到了岸边,但是可怜的安妮却差一点被淹死,幸好那个男人抓住了她。

12. 哈利回到家时快要被冻僵了,他告诉妈妈自己没有听她的话。这个教训令他终生难忘。

LESSON 16
BIRD FRIENDS

——◇——

鸟类的朋友

wife	*greet*	*beard*	*worms*	*prayers*
faith	*grove*	*crusts*	*church*	*furnished*

1. I once knew a man who was rich in his love for birds, and in their love for him. He lived in the midst of a grove full of all kinds of trees. He had no wife or children in his home.

2. He was an old man with gray beard, blue and kind eyes, and a voice that the birds loved; and this was the way he made them his friends.

3. While he was at work with a rake on his nice walks in the grove, the birds came close to him to pick up the worms in the fresh earth he dug up. At first, they kept a rod or two from him, but they soon found he was a kind man, and would not hurt them, but liked to have them near him.

4. They knew this by his kind eyes and voice, which tell what is in the heart. So, day by day their faith in his love grew in them.

5. They came close to the rake. They would hop on top of it to be first at the worm. They would turn up their eyes into his when he spoke to them, as if they said, "He is a kind man; he loves us; we need not fear him."

6. All the birds of the grove were soon his fast friends. They were on the watch for him, and would fly down from the green tree tops to greet him with their chirp.

7. When he had no work on the walks to do with his rake or his hoe, he took crusts of bread with him, and dropped the crumbs on the ground. Down they would dart on his head and feet to catch them as they fell from his hand.

8 He showed me how they loved him. He put a crust of bread in his mouth, with one end of it out of his lips. Down they came like bees at a flower, and flew off with it crumb by crumb.

9. When they thought he slept too long in the morning, they would fly in and sit on the bedpost, and call him up with their chirp.

10. They went with him to church, and while he said his prayers and sang his hymns in it, they sat in the trees, and sang their praises to the same good God who cares for them as he does for us.

11. Thus the love and trust of birds were a joy to him all his life long; and such love and trust no boy or girl can fail to win with the same kind heart, voice, and eye that he had.

(*Elihu Burritt*)

【中文阅读】

1. 我曾经认识一个朋友，他非常喜欢小鸟，甚至可以说是深爱着它们。他住在一片茂密的小树林里，家中无妻无子，就他一人。

2. 他是一位和蔼善良的老人家，长着灰白的胡须、蓝色的眼睛和所有小鸟都喜欢的声音。正是因为这个原因，他才和小鸟成了朋友。

3. 当他在美丽的林中小路上用耙子工作时，小鸟都会飞来接近他，从刚挖掘出的新鲜泥土上拣拾虫子吃。起先，它们会和他保持距离，足有一两根秆子那么远，但是很快地，它们发现这是一个友好和蔼的老人，不会伤害自己，而且还喜欢接近自己。

4. 通过老人家慈祥的眼神和温柔的声音，它们了解了他的心声。于是，一天天地，小鸟越来越相信老人家是自己的朋友，越来越相信他对自己的爱与日俱增。

5. 它们慢慢地开始靠近犁耙，并且跳上耙子顶端争先恐后地靠近虫子。当他和小鸟说话时，它们也会转动着小眼睛看他，仿佛在说："这是一个慈祥善良的人，他爱我们；我们没必要害怕他。"

6. 很快，小树林里所有的小鸟都成了他可靠的朋友。它们站在枝头观察他，也会从枝繁叶茂的树上飞下来，用唧唧喳喳的啁啾声和他打招呼。

7. 当他不用犁耙和锄头在小路上工作时，就会将带来的硬面包碾成碎屑，丢在地上。就在面包屑从他手中滑掉落的刹那，小鸟们纷纷从天而降，由头到脚地扑向他。

8. 他又用行动表明了小鸟是多么爱他。他将一块面包皮放入嘴中，让另一端留在嘴唇外面。结果，小鸟们又再次像蜜蜂扑花一样从天而降，一块一块地叼走了露在他嘴唇外面的面包渣。

9. 清晨，当小鸟们认为他在睡懒觉时，会飞进屋里坐在床柱上，用唧唧喳喳的声音叫醒他。

10. 它们还和他一起去教堂，当他念诵祈祷词、唱诵赞美诗时，它们就坐在树上，向如他一样眷顾自己的上帝唱诵赞美诗。

11. 因此，对他来说，这种对小鸟的爱和信任就是一种终生的喜悦；而且，这种爱和信任是任何一个男孩或女孩都无法以如他那样慈善的心、声音和眼神而赢得的。

（伊莱休·伯里特）

LESSON 17
WHAT THE MINUTES SAY

◇

———— ◇ ————

分针之语

1. We are but minutes—little things!
   Each one furnished with sixty wings,
   With which we fly on our unseen track,
   And not a minute ever comes back.

2. We are but minutes; use us well,
   For how we are used we must one day tell.
   Who uses minutes, has hours to use;
   Who loses minutes, whole years must lose.

【中文阅读】

1. 我们不过是分钟而已——微不足道！
   每一分钟都配有六十个羽翼，
   我们以此隐形翅膀，沿着看不见的轨道飞翔，
   没有一分钟曾经逆转。

2. 我们只不过是分钟而已，充分利用我们吧，
   我们必须告知世人如何加以利用。
   那些充分利用每分钟的人，总有许多小时可用；
   那些让失去分钟的人，可能会让一整年溜走。

LESSON 18

THE WIDOW AND THE MERCHANT

◇

寡妇和商人

died   *woman*   *convinced*   *amazed*   *wrote*

pity   *mistake*   *rewarded*   *grateful*   *check*

distress   *hesitation*

husband   *musician*

widow   *assistance*

1. A merchant, who was very fond of music, was asked by a poor widow to give her some assistance. Her husband, who was a musician, had died, and left her very poor indeed.

2. The merchant saw that the widow and her daughter, who was with her, were in great distress. He looked with pity into their pale faces, and was

49

convinced by their conduct that their sad story was true.

3. "How much do you want, my good woman?" said the merchant.

4. "Five dollars will save us," said the poor widow, with some hesitation.

5. The merchant sat down at his desk, took a piece of paper, wrote a few lines on it, and gave it to the widow with the words, "Take it to the bank you see on the other side of the street."

6. The grateful widow and her daughter, without stopping to read the note, hastened to the bank. The banker at once counted out fifty dollars instead of five, and passed them to the widow.

7. She was amazed when she saw so much money. "Sir, there is a mistake here," she said. "You have given me fifty dollars, and I asked for only five."

8. The banker looked at the note once more, and said, "The check calls for fifty dollars."

9. "It is a mistake—indeed it is," said the widow.

10. The banker then asked her to wait a few minutes, while he went to see the merchant who gave her the note.

11. "Yes." said the merchant, when he had heard the banker's story, "I did make a mistake. I wrote fifty instead of five hundred. Give the poor widow five hundred dollars, for such honesty is poorly rewarded with even that sum."

【中文阅读】

1. 有一个商人很喜欢音乐，一个可怜的穷寡妇曾经向他求助。她的丈夫是一个音乐家，可惜英年早逝，给她留下了少得可怜的财产。

2. 商人注意到，这个寡妇和她身边的女儿极其贫困。他很同情地看着寡妇那苍白的脸，心中已被她们的行为说服了，对她们那悲伤的故事信以为真。

3. "你想要多少钱，夫人？"商人说。

4. "5美元就能救救我们了。"这个可怜的寡妇略带犹疑地说。

5. 商人坐在桌前，拿出一张纸，写下了几行字，然后递给寡妇，说："把它拿到街对面的那家银行去换钱吧。"

6. 感激不尽的寡妇和女儿甚至都没有认真看字条，就急忙赶到了银行。银行里的职员并没有给她五美元，而是立刻数出了五十美元，递到这个寡妇手里。

7. 看到这么多钱，她惊呆了。"先生，是不是弄错了，"她说，"您给了我五十美元，而我只要了五美元。"

8. 银行里的职员马上又看了一下支票，说："这是一张五十美元的支票。"

9. 寡妇又说："那一定是弄错了。"

10. 银行职员让她耐心等几分钟，然后就去找开出支票的商人。

11. 当商人听完银行职员的叙述后，说："是的，我犯了一个错误。我只写下了五十美元，而不是五百美元。给那个可怜的寡妇五百美元吧，因为这种诚实的美德多少钱也换不来。"

LESSON 19

THE BIRDS SET FREE

◆

小鸟自由了

wires	*trade*	*bargain*	*sadness*	*prisoners*
war	*French*	*apiece*	*number*	*resolved*

1. A man was walking one day through a large city. On a street corner he saw a boy with a number of small birds for sale, in a cage.

2. He looked with sadness upon the little prisoners flying about the cage, peeping through the wires, beating them with their wings, and trying to get out.

3. He stood for some time looking at the birds. At last he said to the boy, "How much do you ask for your birds?"

4. "Fifty cents apiece, sir," said the boy. "I do not mean how much apiece,"

said the man, "but how much for all of them? I want to buy them all."

5. The boy began to count, and found they came to five dollars. "There is your money," said the man. The boy took it, well pleased with his morning's trade.

6. No sooner was the bargain settled than the man opened the cage door, and let all the birds fly away.

7. The boy, in great surprise, cried, "What did you do that for, sir? You have lost all your birds."

8. "I will tell you why I did it," said the man. "I was shut up three years in a French prison, as a prisoner of war, and I am resolved never to see anything in prison which I can make free."

【中文阅读】

1. 有一天，一位绅士在一座大城市里穿行。走到一个街角，他看到一个小男孩在兜售笼子里的小鸟。

2. 他忧郁地看着那些囚犯似的小鸟在笼子里飞来飞去，透过网格传出了唧唧喳喳地叫声，它们不停地拍打着翅膀，努力想飞出去。

3. 他在那里站了一会儿，一直看着这些小鸟。最后，他对小男孩说："这些鸟，你卖多少钱？"

4. "五毛钱一只，先生，"小男孩说。"我没问你多少钱一只，"这个男人说，"我想知道这一笼鸟卖多少钱？我想买下所有的鸟。"

5. 小男孩开始计数，最后发现这些鸟能卖五美元。"这是给你的钱，"这个男人说。男孩接过了钱，很高兴能在早上有这样一桩买卖。

6. 就在交易成功的一刹那，这个男人立刻打开了鸟笼的门，所有的鸟儿立刻倾巢而出。

7. 男孩惊讶极了，大喊道："先生，您在做什么呀？您失去了所有的鸟。"

8. 这个男人说："我会告诉你这样做的原因。作为一个战犯，我在一所法国监狱里被囚禁了三年，而且我下定决心，只要我能做到，绝不会再看到任何一个人被关进监狱。"

LESSON 20
A MOMENT TOO LATE

为时已晚

downy   *firmly*   *staid*   *petals*   *crime*

1. A moment too late, my beautiful bird,
   A moment too late are you now;
   The wind has your soft, downy nest disturbed—
   The nest that you hung on the bough.

2. A moment too late; that string in your bill,
   Would have fastened it firmly and strong;
   But see, there it goes, rolling over the hill!
   Oh, you staid a moment too long.

3. A moment, one moment too late, busy bee;
   The honey has dropped from the flower:
   No use to creep under the petals and see;
   It stood ready to drop for an hour.

4. A moment too late; had you sped on your wing,
   The honey would not have been gone;
   Now you see what a very, a very sad thing
   'T is to stay a moment too long.

5. Little girl, never be a moment too late,
   It will soon end in trouble or crime;

Better be an hour early, and stand and wait,
　　Than a moment behind the time.

6. If the bird and the bee, little boy, were too late,
　　Remember, as you play along
On your way to school, with pencil and slate,
　　Never stay a moment too long.

【中文阅读】

1. 仅只迟了一点，我漂亮的小鸟，
　你只是晚了那么一点点，
　你悬挂在树枝上柔软温暖的巢，
　已被风吹毁不见。

2. 只是迟了一点点，你嘴上的绳线，
　本来可以把巢紧紧绑牢；
　可是你看，它已滚落到山那边！
　噢，你逗留的时间短一点点多好。

3. 一点点，忙碌的蜜蜂就迟了一点点，
　花朵上的蜜已经滴落在地；
　现在再也不必爬到花瓣下察看，
　它在那儿摇摇欲坠足有一小时。

4. 只是迟了一点点，如果快点扇动翅膀，
　蜂蜜就不会消失；
　你看这事多么令人伤心，
　哪怕它再多停留一下子。

5. 小宝贝，千万不要迟到，哪怕一点点，
   瞬间也会招致恶果或麻烦；
   宁可提早一小时站立等候，
   胜过落后迟到一点点。

6. 小男孩，如果小鸟和蜜蜂为时太晚，
   记住，当你在上学途中玩耍流连，
   带着你的铅笔和小石板
   千万不要停留太久，哪怕只是一点点。

LESSON 21
HUMMING BIRDS

———◇———

蜂　鸟

West Indies　*adorn*　　*approach*　*motion*　*attached*
sugar plum　*cotton*　　*instinct*　*object*　*defending*
necessary　*rapid*　　*brilliant*　*fibers*　*severely*

1. The most beautiful humming birds are found in the West Indies and South America. The crest of the tiny head of one of these shines like a sparkling crown of colored light.

2. The shades of color that adorn its breast, are equally brilliant. As the bird flits from one object to another, it looks more like a bright flash of sunlight than it does like a living being.

3. But, you ask, why are they called humming birds? It is because they make a soft, hum-ming noise by the rapid motion of their wings—a motion so rapid, that as they fly you can only see that they have wings.

4. One day when walking in the woods, I found the nest of one of the smallest humming birds. It was about half the size of a very small hen's egg, and was attached to a twig no thicker than a steel knitting needle.

5. It seemed to have been made of cotton fibers, and was covered with the softest bits of leaf and bark. It had two eggs in it, quite white, and each

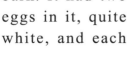

about as large as a small sugarplum.

6. When you approach the spot where one of these birds has built its nest, it is necessary to be careful. The mother bird will dart at you and try to peck your eyes. Its sharp beak may hurt your eyes most severely, and even destroy the sight.

7. The poor little thing knows no other way of defending its young, and instinct teaches it that you might carry off its nest if you could find it.

【中文阅读】

1. 世界上最美丽的蜂鸟仅仅在西印度群岛和南美洲发现过。其中一只小鸟很特别，它的小脑袋上有一个闪烁着耀眼光芒的顶冠，就像色彩斑斓的璀璨皇冠一样。

2. 顶冠也同样照亮了它的胸脯，如同点缀的光影一样。当小鸟从一个地方飞到另一个地方，它看起来就像一道亮闪闪的光，而不是一个活生生的小生命。

3. 然而，您可能会问，它们为何被称为蜂鸟呢？正是因为它们在飞翔时急速扇动翅膀，从而制造出嗡嗡的蜂鸣声，才由此而得名。蜂鸟颤动翅膀的速度极其快，以至于人们只能看到空中翱翔而过的翅膀，反而看不到它的身体。

4. 有一天，当我在林中漫步时，发现了一只小蜂鸟的鸟巢。这个小巢穴大概只有半个鸡蛋大，附着在一根还不如钢针粗的小树枝上。

5. 它看上去就像是用棉线编织成的，上面覆盖着柔软的叶子和树皮。里面有两只小卵，纯白色的，每个卵都像一粒小糖果似的。

6. 当你靠近这类鸟巢时，一定要非常小心。鸟妈妈会向你扑来，试图啄食你的眼睛。它那尖尖的鸟嘴或许会重伤您的眼睛，甚至可能会让您失明。

7. 这个可怜的小东西并不知道除此之外还有什么可以保护幼子的方法，它只会本能地认为，如果您能找到鸟巢，就会夺走它。

LESSON 22

THE WIND AND THE SUN

◇

风和太阳

decide	*buckled*	*mountain*	*shelter*	*party*
dispute	*succeed*	*forcibly*	*mantle*	*oven*

1. A dispute once arose between the Wind and the Sun, as to which was the stronger.

2. To decide the matter, they agreed to try their power on a traveler. That party which should first strip him of his cloak, was to win the day.

3. The Wind began. He blew a cutting blast, which tore up the mountain oaks by their roots, and made the whole forest look like a wreck.

4. But the traveler, though at first he could scarcely keep his cloak on his back, ran under a hill for shelter, and buckled his mantle about him more closely.

5. The Wind having thus tried his utmost power in vain, the Sun began.

6. Bursting through a thick cloud, he darted his sultry beams so forcibly upon the traveler's head, that the poor fellow was almost melted.

7. "This," said he, "is past all bearing. It is so hot, that one might as well be in an oven."

8. So he quickly threw off his cloak, and went into the shade of a tree to cool himself.

9. This fable teaches us, that gentle means will often succeed where forcible ones will fail.

【中文阅读】

1. 有一次，风和太阳起了争执，双方都在强调自己更厉害。

2. 为了解决这个问题，风和太阳都同意在一个旅行者身上施展威力。最先让他脱掉斗篷的一方，就是当天的胜利者。

3. 风先开始，它发动了猛烈地攻击，甚至把山上的橡树都连根拔起来了，整个森林一片狼藉，似乎全都遭到了严重破坏。

4. 但是，这个旅行者起先尽管差点没能保住自己背上的斗篷，但他很快就跑到一个小山丘下寻求庇护，并且迅速紧紧地扣好了身上的斗篷。

5. 风几乎用尽了全部力气，依然徒劳无功，接下来轮到了太阳进攻。

6. 太阳光冲破厚厚的云层喷薄而出，猛烈地向旅行者的头顶照射强光，这个可怜的家伙都快被融化了。

7. 他自言自语地说："再也受不了了，实在太热了，就像在烤箱中一样备受煎熬。"

8. 于是，他快速脱掉了自己的斗篷，走到一片树阴下乘凉。

9. 这则寓言告诉我们，温柔的手段往往会成功，而强硬的手段往往都会失败。

LESSON 23
SUNSET

---◇---

日　落

sinking　　　　*streamlet*　　　　*sweetness*　　　　*cowslip*

Now the sun is sinking
In the golden west;
Birds and bees and children
All have gone to rest;

And the merry streamlet,
    As it runs along,
With a voice of sweetness
    Sings its evening song.

2.

Cowslip, daisy, violet,
    In their little beds,
All among the grasses
    Hide their heavy heads;
There they'll all, sweet darlings,
    Lie in the happy dreams.
Till the rosy morning
    Wakes them with its beams.

LESSON 24
BEAUTIFUL HANDS

◇

美丽的手

opinion   piano   coarse   bathe   sweep

1. "O Miss Roberts! what coarse-looking hands Mary Jessup has!" said Daisy Marvin, as she walked home from school with her teacher.

2. "In my opinion, Daisy, Mary's hands are the prettiest in the class."

3. "Why, Miss Roberts, they are as red and hard as they can be. How they would look if she were to try to play on a piano!" exclaimed Daisy.

4. Miss Roberts took Daisy's hands in hers, and said, "Your hands are

very soft and white, Daisy—just the hands to look beautiful on a piano; yet they lack one beauty that Mary's hands have. Shall I tell you what the difference is?"

5. "Yes, please, Miss Roberts."

6. "Well, Daisy, Mary's hands are always busy. They wash dishes; they make fires; they hang out clothes, and help to wash them, too; they sweep, and dust, and sew; they are always trying to help her poor, hard-working mother.

7. "Besides, they wash and dress the children; they mend their toys and dress their dolls; yet, they find time to bathe the head of the little girl who is so sick in the next house to theirs.

8. "They are full of good deeds to every living thing. I have seen them patting the tired horse and the lame dog in the street. They are always ready to help those who need help."

9. "I shall never think Mary's hands are ugly any more, Miss Roberts."

10. "I am glad to hear you say that, Daisy; and I must tell you that they are beautiful because they do their work gladly and cheerfully."

11. "O Miss Roberts! I feel so ashamed of myself, and so sorry," said Daisy, looking into her teacher's face with tearful eyes.

12. "Then, my dear, show your sorrow by deeds of kindness. The good alone are really beautiful."

【中文阅读】

1. 黛茜·马文和老师一起走在放学回家的路上，她对老师说："噢，罗伯茨小姐！玛丽·吉塞普的手看上去多么粗糙呀！"

2. "黛茜，在我看来，玛丽的手是我们班上最美的手。"

3. "为什么，罗伯茨小姐，她的那双手又红又硬。她那双手将来能弹钢琴吗，会是什么样子呀！"黛茜解释说。

4. 罗伯茨小姐捧起黛茜的手，说："黛茜，你的手非常柔软白皙，正是那种弹钢琴的美丽小手；但是，它们却缺乏玛丽的那双手所展现出的美丽。要我告诉你区别是什么吗？"

5. "是的，请说吧，罗伯茨小姐。"

6. "好吧，黛茜，玛丽的手总是闲不住——既要洗餐具、生火做饭、洗衣服、晒衣服，又要打扫卫生、清扫灰尘、缝补衣服。她的手总想给努力工作的可怜母亲多提供点帮助。"

7. "除此之外，她的双手还要给小孩子洗澡、穿衣服，还要修补玩具、给玩偶穿衣服等；但是，它们依然能抽空去给隔壁邻居家生病的小姑娘洗头。"

8. "对每一个生灵来说，这双手一直在做着善事。我还曾经见过这双手轻轻拍打着疲倦的马驹和大街上跛脚的小狗。这双手总在准备着帮助那些有所需求的对象。"

9. "罗伯茨小姐，我再也不认为玛丽的手丑陋不堪了。"

10. "我很高兴听到你这样说，黛茜；而且我必须要告诉你，正是因为那双手能够欢喜并愉悦地做着这些事情，所以才会如此美丽。"

11. "噢，罗伯茨小姐！我真为自己感到羞愧，我很抱歉！"黛茜一边说着，一边噙着泪珠看了看老师的脸。

12. "那么，亲爱的黛茜，就用仁慈的举动来表明你的懊悔吧。善良的好人都很美丽。"

LESSON 25
THINGS TO REMEMBER

◆

应牢记之事

avoid	*prevent*	*forgive*	*rise*	*guide*
during	*pouting*	*protection*	*slam*	*manner*
peevish	*howling*	*satisfied*	*trust*	*angry*

1. When you rise in the morning, remember who kept you from danger during the night. Remember who watched over you while you slept, and whose sun shines around you, and gives you the sweet light of day.

2. Let God have the thanks of your heart, for his kindness and his care; and pray for his protection during the wakeful hours of day.

3. Remember that God made all creatures to be happy, and will do nothing that may prevent their being so, without good reason for it.

4. When you are at the table, do not eat in a greedy manner, like a pig. Eat quietly, and do not reach forth your hand for the food, but ask some one to help you.

5. Do not become peevish and pout, because you do not get a part of everything. Be satisfied with what is given you.

6. Avoid a pouting face, angry looks, and angry words. Do not slam the doors. Go quietly up and down stairs; and never make a loud noise about the house.

7. Be kind and gentle in your manners; not like the howling winter storm, but like the bright summer morning.

8. Do always as your parents bid you. Obey them with a ready mind, and with a pleasant face.

9. Never do anything that you would be afraid or ashamed that your parents should know. Remember, if no one else sees you, God does, from whom you can not hide even your most secret thought.

10. At night, before you go to sleep, think whether you have done anything that was wrong during the day, and pray to God to forgive you. If anyone has done you wrong, forgive him in your heart.

11. If you have not learned something useful, or been in some way useful, during the past day, think that it is a day lost, and be very sorry for it.

12. Trust in the Lord, and He will guide you in the way of good men. The path of the just is as the shining light that shineth more and more unto the perfect day.

13. We must do all the good we can to all men, for this is well pleasing in the sight of God. He delights to see his children walk in love, and do good one to another.

【中文阅读】

1. 当你早上起床时，要记住那个在夜晚使你免遭危险的人。要记得那个于你熟睡时一直在旁守护的人，那个在你身边光芒四射的人以及那个带给你甜美时光的人。

2. 愿上帝赋予你感恩的心，为了他的仁慈与关爱；并且在你清醒的时候祈求他的护佑。

3. 请记住，上帝让所有生灵都快乐，并且从不会无故地阻止他们获得幸福和快乐。

4. 当你坐在饭桌旁，不要像猪一样贪婪地吃东西。你应安安静静地吃，不要伸出手去拿远处的食物，而应请其他人帮忙取。

5. 不要因为自己事事无份而轻易暴躁生气，要对自己被赋予的一切心满意足。

6. 我们应尽量避免生气、愤怒的面貌和恶毒的话语，更不要猛力敲门。我们应该安静平稳地上下楼梯；永远不要在居家附近制造噪音。

7. 我们应有和善且温柔的礼仪，不要像咆哮的冬日暴雪，而要像阳光明媚的夏日清晨。

8. 当父母对你有所吩咐时，应奉命行事。要带着心甘情愿的心情和愉悦的面容顺从他们。

9. 不要做任何会让自己害怕或羞愧的事情，父母都会了然于胸。请记住，即便无人看到你的所作所为，上帝也会看到；即使你最隐秘的思想，在上帝那里也无处藏身。

10. 入夜，上床前，好好想想白天是否做过什么错事，并且要向上帝祈求原谅。如果有人做了对不起你的事情，那就从心里原谅对方。

11. 在过去的一天里，如果你尚未学到有用的东西，或者未达到某种有用的程度，想想这虚度的一日吧，你应感到万分歉意。

12. 相信上帝，他会引领你走上好人之路。正直就像一道耀眼的光，会使你越来越完美。

13. 我们必须为所有人做一切力所能及的好事，因为这样才会取悦上帝。他喜欢看到自己的孩子在爱中成长，并且善待自己和他人。

LESSON 26
THREE LITTLE MICE

◇

三只小老鼠

exactly	*folding*	*cheese*	*chamber*	*rattling*
protruded	*forepaws*	*gazed*	*doubt*	*released*
perplexed	*lattice*	*queer*	*cozy*	*staircase*

1. I will tell you the story of three little mice,
   If you will keep still and listen to me,
Who live in a cage that is cozy and nice,
   And are just as cunning as cunning can be.
They look very wise, with their pretty red eyes,
   That seem just exactly like little round beads;

They are white as the snow, and stand up in a row
    Whenever we do not attend to their needs;—

2. Stand up in a row in a comical way,—
    Now folding their forepaws as if saying, "please;"
Now rattling the lattice, as much as to say,
    "We shall not stay here without more bread and cheese,"
They are not at all shy, as you'll find, if you try
    To make them run up in their chamber to bed;
If they don't want to go, why, they won't go—ah! no,
    Though you tap with your finger each queer little head.

3. One day as I stood by the side of the cage,
    Through the bars there protruded a funny, round tail;
Just for mischief I caught it, and soon, in a rage,
    Its owner set up a most pitiful wail.
He looked in dismay,—there was something to pay,—
    But what was the matter he could not make out;
What was holding him so, when he wanted to go
    To see what his brothers upstairs were about?

4. But soon from the chamber the others rushed down,
    Impatient to learn what the trouble might be;
I have not a doubt that each brow wore a frown,
    Only frowns on their brows are not easy to see.
For a moment they gazed, perplexed and amazed;
    Then began both together to—gnaw off the tail!
So, quick I released him,—do you think that it pleased him?
    And up the small staircase they fled like a gale.

(Julia C. R. Dorr)

【中文阅读】

1. 如果你能安静好好聆听，
   我会给你讲三只小老鼠的故事。
   它们住在一个舒适惬意的笼子里，
   像普通老鼠那样狡猾精明。
   它们看上去非常聪明，
   眨着可爱的红色小眼睛，
   看上去真像小圆珠子；
   它们身白如雪，
   每当我们忽略其需求时，它们就会站成一排；

2. 他们以令人好笑的方式站成一排，
   合上前爪，仿佛在说："求求你"；
   它们又咔哒咔哒地弄着格子，似乎在说：
   "没有面包和奶酪，我们就不待在这里了"。
   你会发现它们一点儿也不害羞，
   假如你想让它们沿着梯子跑回卧室；
   如果它们不想回去，它们绝不回去呀！
   尽管你用手指敲着它们那奇怪的小脑袋。

3. 一天我站在笼子边，
   栅栏里伸出一条有趣的圆尾巴；
   为了好玩我很快就抓住了它；
   尾巴的主人在笼子里发出了可怜的哀号。
   它看上去很沮丧，似乎要付出代价了
   但是，它不明白问题出在了哪里，
   当它想去看看楼上的兄弟们在做什么时，
   究竟是什么抓住了它？

4. 然而，很快地，另外两只小老鼠从楼上的卧室里冲下来，迫不及待地想了解发生了什么事情；

它们个个都皱着眉头，对此我一点儿都不怀疑，

只不过它们那紧皱着的眉头不太容易被发现罢了。

它们痴痴地凝视了片刻，既惊讶又困惑；

然后，一起过来准备咬断那条尾巴！

于是，我马上就放开了它，你认为它会因此而高兴吗？

它像风一样夹着尾巴快速跑上了小扶梯。

LESSON 27

THE NEW YEAR

◇

新　年

Edward　　*receive*　　*wretched*　　*thousand*　　*gratitude*
repeat　　*language*　　*shivering*　　*German*　　*understood*

1. One pleasant New-year morning, Edward rose, and washed and dressed himself in haste. He wanted to be first to wish a happy New Year.

2. He looked in every room, and shouted the words of welcome. He ran into the street, to repeat them to those he might meet.

3. When he came back, his father gave him two bright, new silver dollars.

4. His face lighted up as he took them. He had wished for a long time to

buy some pretty books that he had seen at the bookstore.

5. He left the house with a light heart, intending to buy the books.

6. As he ran down the street, he saw a poor German family, the father, mother, and three children shivering with cold.

7. "I wish you a happy New Year," said Edward, as he was gayly passing on. The man shook his head.

8. "You do not belong to this country," said Edward. The man again shook his head, for he could not understand or speak our language.

9. But he pointed to his mouth, and to the children, as if to say, "These little ones have had nothing to eat for a long time."

10. Edward quickly understood that these poor people were in distress. He took out his dollars, and gave one to the man, and the other to his wife.

11. How their eyes sparkled with gratitude! They said something in their language, which doubtless meant, "We thank you a thousand times, and will remember you in our prayers."

12. When Edward came home, his father asked what books he had bought. He hung his head a moment, but quickly looked up.

13. "I have bought no books," said he, "I gave my money to some poor people, who seemed to be very hungry and wretched."

14. "I think I can wait for my books till next New Year. Oh, if you had seen how glad they were to receive the money!"

15. "My dear boy," said his father, "here is a whole bundle of books. I give them to you, more as a reward for your goodness of heart than as a New-year gift.

16. "I saw you give the money to the poor German family. It was no small sum for a little boy to give cheerfully.

17. "Be thus ever ready to help the poor, and wretched, and distressed; and every year of your life will be to you a happy New Year."

【中文阅读】

1. 新年第一天，这是一个令人愉快的清晨，爱德华起床后匆忙地梳洗、穿衣。他想成为第一个去祝贺新年快乐的人。

2. 他大声说着喜迎新年的话，冲进每个房间。然后，他又跑到街上，向每一个见到的人问候新年快乐。

3. 回家后，爸爸给了他两枚锃亮的新银元。

4. 拿到这些银币，他的脸上立刻光彩照人。许久以来，他一直想去书店里买那些早已看好的书。

5. 他满怀喜悦地离开家，准备去买书。

6. 跑到街上后，他看到了一家贫穷可怜的德国人，爸爸、妈妈和三个孩子都在寒风中瑟瑟发抖。

7. "祝你们新年快乐！"爱德华带着愉快的心情从他们身旁经过。这个男人摇了摇头。

8. 爱德华问道："你不是本国人。"这个男人继续摇着头，因为他根本不明白爱德华说的话，又或者他不会讲我们的语言。

9. 但是，他指了指自己的嘴，然后又指了指孩子们的嘴，仿佛在说："这些小家伙很久没吃东西了。"

10. 爱德华马上明白了，这些可怜人遇到了困难。他拿出自己刚得到的钱，取出一块银币给了那个男人，另一块给了他的妻子。

11. 感激之情从他们的眼中流露出来！他们用自己的母语说了些什么，毫无疑问，他们可能在说："我们真是万分地感激你，我们将永远记得你，为你祝福。"

12. 爱德华回家后，爸爸问他买了些什么书。他低下了头，但是很快就抬了起来。

13. "我没有买书，"他说，"我把钱给了一些穷人，他们看上去又冷又饿，一副悲惨的样子。"

14. "我想，我可以等到下一个新年再去买书。哦，要是你看到他们收到钱时高兴的样子就好了！"

15. "我的好孩子，"爸爸说，"这里有一捆书，我全都给你，这是对你的回报，如此善举的意义远远超过了任何新年礼物。"

16. "我看到你把钱给那家可怜的德国人了。只要能够高高兴兴地施与，对一个小男孩来说，钱多钱少都不重要。"

17. "就这样时刻准备着帮助穷苦之人、不幸之人、痛苦贫困之人；你生命中的每一年都会快乐幸福。"

LESSON 28
THE CLOCK AND THE SUNDIAL

◇

时钟与日晷

stock	*spirit*	*humble*	*gloomy*	*sundial*
folly	*steeple*	*stupid*	*boasting*	*modesty*

1. One gloomy day, the clock on a church steeple, looking down on a sundial, said, "How stupid it is in you to stand there all the while like a stock!

2. "You never tell the hour till a bright sun looks forth from the sky, and gives you leave. I go merrily round, day and night, in summer and winter the same, without asking his leave.

3. "I tell the people the time to rise, to go to dinner, and to come to church.

4. "Hark! I am going to strike now; one, two, three, four. There it is for you. How silly you look! You can say nothing."

5. The sun, at that moment, broke forth from behind a cloud, and showed, by the sundial, that the clock was half an hour behind the right time.

6. The boasting clock now held his tongue, and the dial only smiled at his folly.

7. MORAL.—Humble modesty is more often right than a proud and boasting spirit.

【中文阅读】

1. 在一个阴霾的日子里，教堂塔尖上的时钟俯视着下面的日晷，说："你真傻，就像树干似的一直站在那里！"

2. "只有当明亮的太阳从空中直射到你，并且给予许可时，你才会计时，否则，你永远也不可能说出时间。而我就在愉快地绕行，无论春夏秋冬，都在夜以继日地工作，从来不需要得到太阳的允许。"

3. "我能告诉人们何时该起床，何时该出去吃饭，何时该到教堂来了。"

4. "听！我现在该报时了；一，二，三，四。这是给你听的。你看上去多么愚蠢呀！什么也不会说！"

5. 就是那时，太阳从一片云彩后面喷薄而出，通过日晷显示出时钟走慢了半个小时。

6. 正在吹嘘的时钟这下可住了嘴，日晷转盘只是对它笑了笑而已。

7. 寓意——谦虚、谦卑往往比浮夸的骄傲与吹嘘更真实确切。

LESSON 29
REMEMBER

---◇---

记　住

punish　　*actions*　　*wicked*　　*falsehood*　　*wakeful*

1. Remember, child, remember,
   That God is in the sky;
   That He looks down on all we do,
   With an ever-wakeful eye.

2. Remember, oh remember,
   That, all the day and night,
   He sees our thoughts and actions
   With an ever-watchful sight.

3. Remember, child, remember,
   That God is good and true;
   That He wishes us to always be
   Like Him in all we do.

4. Remember that He ever hates
   A falsehood or a lie;
   Remember He will punish, too,
   The wicked, by and by.

5. Remember, oh remember,
   That He is like a friend,

And wishes us to holy be,
And happy, in the end.

6. Remember, child, remember,
To pray to Him in heaven;
And if you have been doing wrong,
Oh, ask to be forgiven.

7. Be sorry, in your little prayer,
And whisper in his ear;
Ask his forgiveness and his love.
And He will surely hear.

8. Remember, child, remember,
That you love, with all your might,
The God who watches o'er us,
And gives us each delight;
Who guards us ever through the day,
And saves us in the night.

【中文阅读】

1. 记住，我的孩子，请记住，
上帝一直在天上；
以其清明的眼睛，
关注着我们的一举一动。

2. 记住，我的孩子，请记住，
他以清明之眼，
看透我们的思想和行为，
无论白天还是黑夜。

3. 记住，我的孩子，请记住吧，
    上帝仁慈又正确；
    他希望我们也能
    时刻如他一样。

4. 记住他永远憎恨，
    欺骗或谎言；
    请记住，他也逐渐会
    惩罚那些邪恶。

5. 记住，噢，一定要记住，
    他就像一个朋友，
    希望我们最终能获得
    快乐与圣洁。

6. 记住吧，我的孩子，一定要记住，
    向天堂里的上帝祈祷；
    假如你已经犯下过错，
    那就乞求他的原谅。

7. 在他耳边低语你的祷告，
    充满悔恨和遗憾；
    请求他的谅解和慈爱。
    他一定能听到。

8. 记住吧，我的孩子，一定要记住，
    将你全部的爱，
    给予一直在关注我们、
    赋予我们欢乐的上帝；
    他日夜守护着我们，
    拯救着我们。

LESSON 30

COURAGE AND COWARDICE

◇

勇敢与懦弱

deal	*straight*	*courage*	*reproach*	*cowardice*
depth	*effort*	*coward*	*deserved*	*schoolmates*

1. Robert and Henry were going home from school, when, on turning a corner, Robert cried out, "A fight! let us go and see!"

2. "No," said Henry; "let us go quietly home and not meddle with this quarrel. We have nothing to do with it, and may get into mischief."

3. "You are a coward, and afraid to go," said Robert, and off he ran. Henry went straight home, and in the afternoon went to school, as usual.

4. But Robert had told all the boys that Henry was a coward, and they

laughed at him a great deal.

5. Henry had learned, however, that true courage is shown most in bearing reproach when not deserved, and that he ought to be afraid of nothing but doing wrong.

6. A few days after, Robert was bathing with some schoolmates, and got out of his depth. He struggled, and screamed for help, but all in vain.

7. The boys who had called Henry a coward, got out of the water as fast as they could, but they did not even try to help him.

8. Robert was fast sinking, when Henry threw off his clothes, and sprang into the water. He reached Robert just as he was sinking the last time.

9. By great effort, and with much danger to himself, he brought Robert to the shore, and thus saved his life.

10. Robert and his schoolmates were ashamed at having called Henry a coward. They owned that he had more courage than any of them.

11. Never be afraid to do good, but always fear to do evil.

【中文阅读】

1. 罗伯特和亨利走在放学回家的路上，就在路口拐弯处，罗伯特大声喊道："有人在打架！我们去看看吧！"

2. 亨利说："不去，我们还是老老实实地回家，不要被这类吵架事件牵扯。我们不但帮不上什么忙，或许还会更加添乱。"

3. "你是个胆小鬼，不敢去是吧，"罗伯特说完，自己一个人跑开了。亨利径自回家，下午还是照常去学校上课。

4. 但是，罗伯特却告诉其他小孩子——亨利是个胆小鬼，他们都在嘲笑他。

5. 不过，亨利了解真正的勇敢是在忍受本不应得的耻辱时表现出来的，而且他并没有做坏事，理应无畏无惧。

6. 几天后，罗伯特正和同学们在一个水池中洗澡，不自觉地浸入到深水区。他挣扎着，大声地求救，但是一切都徒劳。

7. 那些叫亨利胆小鬼的孩子们都尽快地跑了出来，甚至没有一个人想到去帮助他。

8. 罗伯特正在迅速下沉，此时，亨利脱下衣服，跳入水中。就在罗伯特将要沉下去的一刹那，亨利抓住了他。

9. 经过努力，亨利不顾个人安危地将罗伯特拉至岸边，就这样拯救了他的生命。

10. 罗伯特和同学们都对自己称呼亨利是个胆小鬼而感到很羞愧。他们承认亨利比任何一个男孩子都勇敢。

11. 永远不要惧怕做好事，但总要当心别做恶事。

LESSON 31

WEIGHING AN ELEPHANT

◇

称 象

eastern	*deliverance*	*weight*	*favorite*	*clever*
sailor	*enormous*	*court*	*quantity*	*subject*
expense	*elephant*	*stroked*	*machine*	*leaning*
opening	*difficulty*	*risen*	*relieved*	*empty*

1. "An eastern king," said Teddy's mother, "had been saved from some great danger. To show his gratitude for deliverance, he vowed he would give to the poor the weight of his favorite elephant in silver."

2. "Oh! what a great quantity that would be," cried Lily, opening her eyes very wide. "But how could you weigh an elephant?" asked Teddy, who was a quiet, thoughtful boy.

3. "There was the difficulty," said his mother. "The wise and learned men of the court stroked their long beards, and talked the matter over, but no one found out how to weigh the elephant.

4. "At last, a poor old sailor found safe and simple means by which to weigh the enormous beast. The thousands and thousands of pieces of silver were counted out to the people; and crowds of the poor were relieved by the clever thought of the sailor."

5. "O mamma," said Lily, "do tell us what it was!"

6. "Stop, stop!" said Teddy. "I want to think for myself—think hard— and find out how an elephant's weight could be known, with little trouble and expense."

7. "I am well pleased," said his mother, "that my little boy should set his mind to work on the subject. If he can find out the sailor's secret before

night, he shall have that orange for his pains."

8. The boy thought hard and long. Lily laughed at her brother's grave looks, as he sat leaning his head on his hands. Often she teased him with the question, "Can you weigh an elephant, Teddy?"

9. At last, while eating his supper, Teddy suddenly cried out, "I have it now!"

10. "Do you think so?" asked his mother.

11. "How would you do it," asked Lily.

12. "First, I would have a big boat brought very close to the shore, and would have planks laid across, so that the elephant could walk right into it."

13. "Oh, such a great, heavy beast would make it sink low in the water," said Lily.

14. "Of course it would," said her brother. "Then I would mark on the outside of the boat the exact height to which the water had risen all around it while the elephant was inside. Then he should march on shore, leaving the boat quite empty."

15. "But I don't see the use of all this," said Lily.

16. "Don't you?" cried Teddy, in surprise. "Why, I should then bring the heaps of silver, and throw them into the boat till their weight would sink it to the mark made by the elephant. That would show that the weight of each was the same."

17. "How funny!" cried Lily; "you would make a weighing machine of the boat?"

18. "That is my plan," said Teddy.

19. "That was the sailor's plan," said his mother. "You have earned the orange, my boy;" and she gave it to him with a smile.

【中文阅读】

1. 泰迪的妈妈说："东方世界中曾经有一个国王临危获救。为了表达自己的感激之情，他发誓要给穷人分发银子，银子的数量就和他最喜欢的大象一样重。"

2. "哇，那可是一笔数目不小的钱呀，"莉丽睁大双眼，大喊道。在一旁陷入沉思的泰迪百思不得其解，便问道："但是，你如何给大象称重量呀？"

3. 妈妈接着说："是有点困难，朝廷上那些智者和有学问的人都在抚摸着自己的长胡子，相互探讨如何称象，可是，没有人能说出具体的衡量方法。"

4. "最后，一个贫穷的老水手找出了安全又简单的方法，可以称到这头巨兽的重量。成千上万的白银被清点出来准备分发给穷人，这个水手的聪明智慧减轻了大批穷人的负担。"

5. 莉丽说："噢，妈妈，快告诉我们是什么方法！"

6. 可泰迪却说："不要，不要！我想自己思考，仔细地想一想，哪怕会有麻烦和损失，我也要自己找出称象的方法。"

7. 他的妈妈说："我很高兴，我的小儿子应该自己动脑筋解决问题。如果他能在今晚找出水手称象的秘密，就可以得到那个橘子作为奖赏了。"

8. 这个男孩子认真地想了很久。当他以手托腮坐在那里时，莉丽还嘲笑哥哥那一本正经的严肃样。她经常用这样的话来取笑他："泰迪，你能称一头大象吗？"

9. 后来，就在吃晚饭时，泰迪突然大喊道："我终于知道了！"

10. "你确定吗？"妈妈问他。

11. 莉丽也问道："你想怎么称呀。"

12. "首先，我需要有一艘大船，能够非常接近岸边，并且还要铺上木板以便能从岸上登船，这样，大象就能直接走上去了。"

13. "哇，像这么体态肥硕的巨兽一定会让船沉下去的。"莉丽说。

14. "当然会了，"她的哥哥说，"接着，我就会在船舷一侧标出大象站在船上时确切的水面高度。然后，让它走上岸，让空船静止下来。"

15. "我可不认为这样做有什么用。"莉丽说。

16. 泰迪吃惊地大喊："你认为没用吗？为什么，我还会把大批白银放到船上，直到它们的重量使船下沉到那个称大象时的刻度。这样就能显示出它们的重量相等了。"

17. "多么有趣呀！你会做出一个和船一样的秤重机吗？"

18. "这还真是我的计划。"泰迪说。

19. "这也正是水手的方案，"他的妈妈说，"我的儿子，你赢得了橘子。"她微笑着把橘子给了泰迪。

LESSON 32

THE SOLDIER

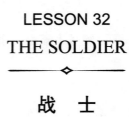

战 士

ranks   *glory*   *arrayed*   *weapons*   *living*
clad   *armor*   *victory*   *contest*   *battle*
blood   *enlist*   *mustered*   *longing*   *warrior*

1. A soldier! a soldier! I'm longing to be:
   The name and the life of a soldier for me!
   I would not be living at ease and at play;
   True honor and glory I'd win in my day.

2. A soldier! a soldier! in armor arrayed;
   My weapons in hand, of no contest afraid;
   I'd ever be ready to strike the first blow,
   And to fight my way through the ranks of the foe.

3. But then, let me tell you, no blood would I shed,
   No victory seek o'er the dying and dead;
   A far braver soldier than this would I be;
   A warrior of Truth, in the ranks of the free.

4. A soldier! a soldier! Oh, then, let me be!
   My friends, I invite you, enlist now with me.
   Truth's bands shall be mustered, love's foes shall give way!
   Let's up, and be clad in our battle array!

(J. G. Adams)

1. 战士！战士！我渴望：
   以战士的名义过着战士的生活，
   我将不再安逸度生、自在玩乐；
   我将赢得生命中真正的荣光和骄傲。

2. 战士！战士！身披铠甲；
   手握钢枪，心无恐惧；
   我已整装待发，
   杀入敌人的队伍。

3. 但我告诉你，没有血途，
   我绝不在死亡中寻找胜利；
   我要成为一个更加勇敢的战士；
   在自由之列中为真理而战的勇士。

4. 战士！战士！噢，让我成为这样一位战士吧！
   我的朋友，我邀请你，和我一起入伍，
   为真理而战的队伍正在集结，
   爱的敌人将会闻风而逃！
   起来吧，加入到我们的斗争之列中！

（J·G·亚当斯）

LESSON 33
THE ECHO

◆

回 声

thicket   *harshly*   *wrath*   *whence*   *rambling*
proving   *toward*   *echo*   *mocking*   *angrily*
foolish   *abroad*   *cross*   *Bible*   *instantly*

1. As Robert was one day rambling about, he happened to cry out, "Ho, ho!" He instantly heard coming back from a hill near by, the same words, "Ho, ho!"

2. In great surprise, he said with a loud voice, "Who are you?" Upon this, the same words came back, "Who are you?"

3. Robert now cried out harshly, "You must be a very foolish fellow."

"Foolish fellow!" came back from the hill.

4. Robert became angry, and with loud and fierce words went toward the spot whence the sounds came. The words all came back to him in the same angry tone.

5. He then went into the thicket, and looked for the boy who, as he thought, was mocking him; but he could find nobody anywhere.

6. When he went home, he told his mother that some boy had hid himself in the wood, for the purpose of mocking him.

7. "Robert," said his mother, "you are angry with yourself alone. You heard nothing but your own words."

8. "Why, mother, how can that be?" said Robert. "Did you never hear an echo?" asked his mother. "An echo, dear mother? No, ma'am. What is it?"

9. "I will tell you," said his mother. "You know, when you play with your ball, and throw it against the side of a house, it bounds back to you." "Yes, mother," said he, "and I catch it again."

10. "Well," said his mother, "if I were in the open air, by the side of a hill or a large barn, and should speak very loud, my voice would be sent back, so that I could hear again the very words which I spoke.

11. "That, my son, is an echo. When you thought some one was mocking you, it was only the hill before you, echoing, or sending back, your own voice.

12. "The bad boy, as you thought it was, spoke no more angrily than yourself. If you had spoken kindly, you would have heard a kind reply.

13. "Had you spoken in a low, sweet, gentle tone, the voice that came back would have been as low, sweet, and gentle as your own.

14. "The Bible says, 'A soft answer turneth away wrath.' Remember this when you are at play with your schoolmates.

15. "If any of them should be offended, and speak in a loud, angry tone, remember the echo, and let your words be soft and kind.

16. "When you come home from school, and find your little brother cross and peevish, speak mildly to him. You will soon see a smile on his lips, and find that his tones will become mild and sweet.

17. "Whether you are in the fields or in the woods, at school or at play, at home or abroad, remember,

The good and the kind,
By kindness their love ever proving,
Will dwell with the pure and the loving."

【中文阅读】

1. 有一天，罗伯特在外面闲逛，他突然大喊："嗨，嗨！"立刻，他就听到附近山上传来了同样的声音，"嗨，嗨！"

2. 更让他大为吃惊的是，当他大声说"你是谁"时，又传来了同样的声音："你是谁？"

3. 接着，罗伯特更加严厉地喊道："你一定是个傻瓜。"山谷中又传回了同样的声音："傻瓜！"

4. 罗伯特开始生气了，用更大的声音、更尖刻的话语冲着那个声音的发源地大喊。这些话语再次以同样的愤怒声调传回到他的耳中。

5. 接着，他跑进灌木丛中，到处去找那个自以为正在嘲笑自己的小男孩；但是，什么人也没有看到。

6. 回到家后，他对妈妈说，有些小男孩为了嘲笑他而隐藏在树林里了。

7. "罗伯特，"妈妈说，"你其实是在对自己生气呢。除了你自己说的话之外，你并没有听到其他人说的话。"

8. 罗伯特问："为什么，妈妈，怎么可能呢？"他的妈妈回答说："你难道从没听说过回声？""亲爱的妈妈，这是回声？不，夫人。这究竟是怎么回事呢？"

9. 妈妈对他说："我来告诉你，知道吗，当你玩球时，对着房子的一面墙扔过去，它会再反弹回来，是吧。""是的，妈妈，"他说，"我会再次接住它。"

10. 他的妈妈说："是的，如果我在一个空旷的地方，在山的一侧或者在一个大谷仓的一边大声地喊，我的声音也会被送回来，这样我就能再次听到那些自己说过的话了。"

11. "孩子，这就是回声。当你认为有人在嘲笑你时，正是面前的大山产生了回响，把你的声音又传了回来。"

12."你想象中的那个坏孩子，也不会比你更生气。如果你说些友好的话，就能听到一个友好的回答了。"

13."如果你用低沉、甜美、温柔的声调说话，那个声音也会像你发出的声音一样低沉、甜美和温柔。"

14."《圣经》里说，'柔和的回答可以消除愤怒。'你和同学们玩耍时一定要记得这些话。"

15."如果他们当中任何一个人正在生气，用愤怒的声调大声讲话，你要记得回声的规律，让自己回应的话语柔和友善。"

16."放学回家时，你若发现小弟弟蛮横暴躁，就温和地同他讲话。很快你就会看到他那充满笑意的嘴角，你还会发现，他的声调也变得温和甜蜜起来。"

17."无论在田野中还是在树林里，无论学习还是玩耍，无论在家中还是在外面，都要记得，好人和善良之人，他们的爱都会通过友好的行为来证明，他们永远都会住在纯洁和爱之中。"

LESSON 34
GEORGE'S FEAST

◇

乔治的美餐

faint	*collect*	*refresh*	*lining*	*happiness*
feast	*scarlet*	*offered*	*lifting*	*strawberries*

1. George's mother was very poor. Instead of having bright, blazing fires in winter, she had nothing to burn but dry sticks, which George picked up from under the trees and hedges.

2. One fine day in July, she sent George to the woods, which were about two miles from the village in which she lived. He was to stay there all day, to get as much wood as he could collect.

3. It was a bright, sunny day, and George worked very hard; so that by

the time the sun was high, he was hot, and wished for a cool place where he might rest and eat his dinner.

4. While he hunted about the bank he saw among the moss some fine, wild strawberries, which were a bright scarlet with ripeness.

5. "How good these will be with my bread and butter!" thought George; and lining his little cap with leaves, he set to work eagerly to gather all he could find, and then seated himself by the brook.

6. It was a pleasant place, and George felt happy and contented. He thought how much his mother would like to see him there, and to be there herself, instead of in her dark, close room in the village.

7. George thought of all this, and just as he was lifting the first strawberry to his mouth, he said to himself, "How much mother would like these;" and he stopped, and put the strawberry back again.

8. "Shall I save them for her?" said he, thinking how much they would refresh her, yet still looking at them with a longing eye.

9. "I will eat half, and take the other half to her," said he at last; and he divided them into two heaps. But each heap looked so small, that he put them together again.

10. "I will only taste one," thought he; but, as he again lifted it to his mouth, he saw that he had taken the finest, and he put it back. "I will keep them all for her," said he, and he covered them up nicely, till he should go home.

11. When the sun was beginning to sink, George set out for home. How happy he felt, then, that he had all his strawberries for his sick mother. The nearer he came to his home, the less he wished to taste them.

12. Just as he had thrown down his wood, he heard his mother's faint voice calling him from the next room. "Is that you, George? I am glad you have come, for I am thirsty, and am longing for some tea."

LEON CUIPON.

95

13. George ran in to her, and joyfully offered his wild strawberries. "And you saved them for your sick mother, did you?" said she, laying her hand fondly on his head, while the tears stood in her eyes. "God will bless you for all this, my child."

14. Could the eating of the strawberries have given George half the happiness he felt at this moment?

【中文阅读】

1. 乔治的妈妈非常贫穷，冬天里见不到明亮、闪烁的炉火，家里没有木柴生火取暖，她只能利用乔治从树下或篱笆边拣来的干树枝取暖。

2. 七月的一天，她让乔治到森林中去拣木头，那个地方离他们住的村子大概两英里远。乔治在森林里逛了一整天，以尽量多收集一点能用的木头。

3. 这是一个洒满阳光的日子，乔治很辛苦地拣拾着木头。等到太阳高高在上时，他已经非常热了，希望能找个凉快的地方吃点东西，好好休息一下。

4. 他一路搜寻到岸边，在苔藓丛中发现了一些外形诱人的野生草莓，散发着明亮的猩红色，一副圆圆的熟透了的样子。

5. "用这些草莓来充当我的面包和奶油，多好呀！"乔治心里这样想着。他将树叶铺在自己的小帽子里，开始迫不及待地去摘那些刚刚发现的草莓，随后，他就在小溪边坐下来。

6. 这是一个很舒适的地方，乔治既高兴又满足。他心想，要是妈妈看到自己坐在这里该多么高兴，她该多么想到这里来坐坐呀，而不是整天待在村中那个黑暗、封闭的小屋里。

7. 乔治一边想着，一边拿起一个草莓准备放入口中，就在这时，他自言自语地说："妈妈该多么喜欢这些草莓呀。"接着，他的手停下来，又把草莓放回原处。

8. "我应该把草莓留给她吗？"他说，心里一边想着这些草莓能给妈妈补充多少营养，一边又带着渴望的眼神看着它们。

9. "我就吃一半，把另一半留给她。"他最后说道；接着，他把草莓分成了两堆。但是，每一堆看上去都那么小，于是，他又把它们合起来。

10."我只尝一个吧，"他心里又想；但是，当他再次拿起草莓放到嘴边时，看到自己拿起了那个最好的草莓，于是他又放了回去。"我还是把草莓都留给她吧，"他一边说着，一边细心地盖好所有草莓，一直留到该回家的时候。

11. 太阳开始下沉时，乔治决定要回家了。他心里多么高兴呀，将所有的草莓都留给了生病的妈妈。越是靠近自己的家，他就越不想去品尝它们了。

12. 刚刚放下拣来的木头，他就听到隔壁房间里传来了妈妈呼唤他的虚弱声音。"是你吗，乔治？我很高兴你回来了，我太渴了，真想能喝点茶。"

13. 乔治立刻跑向她，欢快地把自己采来的野生草莓给妈妈。"你把草莓都留给了生病的妈妈，是吗？"她说，充满怜爱地将手放到乔治头上，眼中噙满了泪水。"上帝会保佑你的，我的孩子。"

14. 自己吃掉草莓，能给乔治带来此刻一半的快乐吗？

LESSON 35
THE LORD'S PRAYER

主祷文

hallow	*amen*	*temptation*	*gracious*
kingdom	*forgive*	*transgressions*	*supplied*
portion	*bounty*	*weakness*	*helpless*
deign	*solemn*	*compassion*	*plumage*
revere	*secure*	*forever*	*pardons*

1. Our Father in heaven,
   We hallow thy name;
   May thy kingdom holy
   On earth be the same;
   Oh, give to us daily
   Our portion of bread;
   It is from thy bounty,
   That all must be fed.

2. Forgive our transgressions.
   And teach us to know
   The humble compassion
   That pardons each foe;
   Keep us from temptation,
   From weakness and sin,
   And thine be the glory
   Forever! Amen!

AN EVENING PRAYER

1.

Before I close my eyes in sleep,
　Lord, hear my evening prayer,
And deign a helpless child to keep,
　With thy protecting care.

2.

Though young in years, I have been taught
　Thy name to love and fear;
Of thee to think with solemn thought;
　Thy goodness to revere.

3.

That goodness gives each simple flower
　Its scent and beauty, too;
And feeds it in night's darkest hour
　With heaven's refreshing dew.

4.

The little birds that sing all day
　In many a leafy wood,
By thee are clothed in plumage gay,
　By thee supplied with food.

5.

And when at night they cease to sing,
　By thee protected still,
Their young ones sleep beneath their wing.

Secure from every ill.

6.

Thus mayst thou guard with gracious arm
The bed whereon I lie,
And keep a child from every harm
By thine own watchful eye.

Bernard Barton

【中文阅读】

1. 我们在天上的父，
   愿人都尊你的名为圣；
   愿你的国降临
   愿你的旨意行在地上如同行在天上；
   我们日用的饮食今日赐给我们；
   来自你的圣恩，
   万民必得喂饲。

2. 不叫我们遇见试探，
   救我脱离凶险。
   因为国度、权柄、荣耀
   全是你的
   直到永远！阿门！

LESSON 36

FINDING THE OWNER

◇

寻找失主

possession	*torment*	*suggested*	*observed*
satisfaction	*thief*	*anxiety*	*finally*
burying	*conscious*	*critical*	*breathless*
experienced	*response*	*evident*	*interfered*

1. "It's mine," said Fred, showing a white handled pocketknife, with every blade perfect and shining. "Just what I've always wanted." And he turned the prize over and over with evident satisfaction.

2. "I guess I know who owns it," said Tom, looking at it with a critical eye.

3. "I guess you don't," was the quick response. "It isn't Mr. Raymond's," said Fred, shooting wide of the mark.

4. "I know that; Mr. Raymond's is twice as large," observed Tom, going on with his drawing lesson.

5. Do you suppose Fred took any comfort in that knife? Not a bit of comfort did he take. He was conscious all the time of having something in his possession that did not belong to him; and Tom's suspicion interfered sadly with his enjoyment.

6. Finally, it became such a torment to him, that he had serious thoughts of burning it, or burying it, or giving it away; but a better plan suggested itself.

7. "Tom," said he, one day at recess, "didn't you say you thought you knew who owned that knife I found?"

8. "Yes, I did; it looked like Doctor Perry's." And Tom ran off to his play, without giving the knife another thought.

9. Dr. Perry's! Why, Fred would have time to go to the doctor's office before recess closed: so he started in haste, and found the old gentleman getting ready to visit a patient. "Is this yours?" cried Fred, in breathless haste, holding up the cause of a week's anxiety.

10. "It was," said the doctor; "but I lost it the other day."

11. "I found it," said Fred, "and have felt like a thief ever since. Here, take it; I've got to run."

12. "Hold on!" said the doctor. "I've got a new one, and you are quite welcome to this."

13. "Am I? May I? Oh! thank you!" And with what a different feeling he kept it from that which he had experienced for a week!

【中文阅读】

1. "这是我的，"弗雷德一边说，一边展示着一把带手柄的白色小刀，刀锋闪闪发亮，非常漂亮。"正是我之前一直想要的。"他将战利品翻来覆去地把玩，带着明显的满足感。

2. "我想，我应该知道它的主人是谁。"汤姆说着，用挑剔的眼神看了一眼这把小刀。

3. "我认为你根本不知道，它根本不是雷蒙德先生的。"弗雷德很快地回答，他的话有点不着边际。

4. "我知道，和雷蒙德先生完全无关。"汤姆一边看着，一边准备去上自己的绘画课。

5. 你认为汤姆拿到这把小刀会很舒服吗？他一点儿也不舒服。他时刻感觉自己占有了本不属于自己的东西；而且，汤姆的疑心也残酷地扰乱了他的快乐。

6. 最后，这竟然变成了他心口的痛，他也曾认真地想过要烧掉它、埋掉它、扔掉它；但是，他又想出了一个更好的主意。

7. 有一天，在休息时，他说："汤姆，你不是说过，你知道这把刀归谁所有吗？"

8. "是的，我知道；看上去像是佩理医生的。"汤姆说完就跑去玩了，根本没再想过这把刀的事。

9. 是佩理医生的！哎呀，在休息时间结束之前，弗雷德完全有时间去医生办公室；于是，他匆忙赶过去，却发现这位老先生正要去看一个病人。"这是您的吗？"弗雷德举着那个使他焦虑不安了一周的罪魁祸首，上气不接下气地喊道。

10. "是的，"医生说，"但是，我已经丢了好几天了。"

11. 弗雷德说："我找到了它，从那以后，我就一直感觉自己像个小偷一样。在这里，拿走吧，我得赶紧回去上课了。"

12. "等一下！"医生说，"我又有了一把新的，你可以留着这把刀。"

13. "我可以吗？噢，非常感谢！"与前一周的感受相比，这种感觉多么与众不同呀！

LESSON 37
BATS

蝙　蝠

immediately

character

squeal

snapped

shunned

quills

terribly

crevices

encountered

prepared

policy

prowling

double

insect

devour

escape

framework　nightmare　disgusting　quadruped

1. Bats are very strange little animals, having hair like mice, and wings like birds. During the day, they live in crevices of rocks, in caves, and in other dark places.

2. At night, they go forth in search of food; and, no doubt, you have seen them flying about, catching such insects as happen to be out rather late at night.

3. The wings of a bat have no quills. They are only thin pieces of skin stretched upon a framework of bones. Besides this, it may be said that while he is a quadruped, he can rise into the air and fly from place to place like a bird.

4. There is a funny fable about the bat, founded upon this double character of beast and bird, which I will tell you.

5. An owl was once prowling about, when he came across a bat. So he

104

caught him in his claws, and was about to devour him. Upon this, the bat began to squeal terribly; and he said to the owl, "Pray, what do you take me for, that you use me thus?"

6. "Why, you are a bird, to be sure," said the owl, "and I am fond of birds. I love dearly to break their little bones."

7. "Well," said the bat, "I thought there was some mistake. I am no bird. Don't you see, Mr. Owl, that I have no feathers, and that I am covered with hair like a mouse?"

8. "Sure enough," said the owl, in great surprise; "I see it now. Really, I took you for a bird, but it appears you are only a kind of mouse. I ate a mouse last night, and it gave me the nightmare. I can't bear mice! Bah! it makes me sick to think of it." So the owl let the bat go.

9. The very next night, the bat encountered another danger. He was snapped up by puss, who took him for a mouse, and immediately prepared to eat him.

10. "I beg you to stop one moment," said the bat. "Pray, Miss Puss, what do you suppose I am?" "A mouse, to be sure!" said the cat. "Not at all," said the bat, spreading his long wings.

11. "Sure enough," said the cat "you seem to be a bird, though your feathers are not very fine. I eat birds sometimes, but I am tired of them just now, having lately devoured four young robins; so you may go. But, bird or

mouse, it will be your best policy to keep out of my way hereafter."

12. The meaning of this fable is, that a person playing a double part may sometimes escape danger; but he is always, like the bat, a creature that is disgusting to everybody, and shunned by all.

(S. G. Goodrich—Adapted)

【中文阅读】

1. 蝙蝠是很奇怪的动物,有着像老鼠一样的毛发和像小鸟一样的翅膀。白天,它们都待在岩石裂缝、洞穴以及其他黑暗的地方。

2. 它们经常在夜里出来觅食,毫无疑问,你可能曾经看见过它们飞来飞去地捕捉那些偶尔在深夜出没的昆虫。

3. 蝙蝠的翅膀并没有羽毛,只有薄薄的皮挂在骨架上。除此之外,据说蝙蝠还有两只脚,它也能像小鸟那样在空中飞来飞去。

4. 基于蝙蝠的这种鸟兽双重特性,还有一个有趣的寓言,我会慢慢告诉你。

5. 有一次,一只猫头鹰在空中徘徊,这时,它看见了一只蝙蝠。于是,它就用爪子抓住了蝙蝠,准备要吞下去。就在这时,蝙蝠可怜巴巴地啼哭着对猫头鹰说:"求求你告诉我,你以为我是谁,为什么抓我呢?"

6. "为什么,你是一只鸟,千真万确,"猫头鹰说,"我很喜欢鸟类,我最爱做的就是弄断它们的小骨头。"

7. 蝙蝠说:"好吧,我想你可能真弄错了。我不是鸟。猫头鹰先生,我并没有羽毛,而且我身上的毛很像老鼠,你没看到吗?"

8. "的确如此,"猫头鹰惊讶地说道,"我现在看清楚了。真的,我以为你是一只鸟呢,但是,从外表看来,你就是一只老鼠。我昨天晚上刚吃了一只老鼠,还让我做了一场噩梦。我再也不吃老鼠了!呸,真让我恶心!"于是,猫头鹰就放走了蝙蝠。

9. 到了第二天,这只蝙蝠又遇到了危险。它被一只花猫逮住了,小花猫把它当成了老鼠,正准备要吃掉它。

10. "求求你,等一下,"这只蝙蝠说,"拜托你告诉我,花猫小姐,你把我当成什么了?""一只老鼠,千真万确!"花猫说。"根本不是。"蝙蝠说着,立刻伸展开它的翅膀。

11. "果真不是呀，"花猫说，"尽管你的翅膀不那么漂亮，但你看上去真像小鸟。我有时也吃小鸟，但我厌倦小鸟，最近已经吃了四只小知更鸟了；所以，你可以走了。但是，不管你是小鸟，还是老鼠，为了保险起见，从今往后最好别再出现在我面前。"

12. 这则寓言故事的意义是，一个两面玲珑的人有时可能会逃脱危险，但他却会像蝙蝠那样遭人厌恶和唾弃。

（S·G· 古德里奇）

LESSON 38
A SUMMER DAY

夏　日

tints　　*sheaves*　　*fireflies*　　*chimney*　　*tinkle*
lawns　　*whirl*　　*buttercup*　　*lowing*　　*lance*

1. This is the way the morning dawns:
　　Rosy tints on flowers and trees,
　　Winds that wake the birds and bees,
　　Dewdrops on the fields and lawns—
This is the way the morning dawns.

2. This is the way the sun comes up:
   Gold on brook and glossy leaves,
   Mist that melts above the sheaves,
   Vine, and rose, and buttercup—
   This is the way the sun comes up.

3. This is the way the river flows:
   Here a whirl, and there a dance;
   Slowly now, then, like a lance,
   Swiftly to the sea it goes—
   This is the way the river flows.

4. This is the way the rain comes down:
   Tinkle, tinkle, drop by drop,
   Over roof and chimney top;
   Boughs that bend, and skies that frown—
   This is the way the rain comes down.

5. This is the way the birdie sings:
   "Baby birdies in the nest,
   You I surely love the best;
   Over you I fold my wings"—
   This is the way the birdie sings.

6. This is the way the daylight dies:
   Cows are lowing in the lane,
   Fireflies wink on hill and plain;
   Yellow, red, and purple skies—
   This is the way the daylight dies.

                                        (*George Cooper*)

【中文阅读】

1. 清晨如此到来：
   花草树木披上玫瑰色的霞光，
   风儿唤醒了小鸟和蜜蜂，
   露珠凝结在田野和草地上——
   黎明这样到来。

2. 太阳如此升起来：
   小溪和绿叶蒙上金色，
   层层薄雾渐渐上升，
   藤蔓、玫瑰花和毛茛露出真容——
   太阳这样升起。

3. 河水如此流淌：
   这里一个漩涡，那里一个跳跃，
   一会舒缓下来，就像一支长矛，
   快速流入大海——
   河水就这样流淌。

4. 雨水如此掉落下来：
   叮当，叮当，一滴一滴…
   掉到屋顶和烟囱帽上，

树枝弯下了腰，天空皱起了眉——
雨水就这样滴落。

5. 小鸟如此歌唱：
"巢里的鸟宝宝，
无疑是我的最爱；
用我的翅膀拥抱你"——
小鸟这样吟唱。

6. 日光如此消失下去：
牛群在小路上哞哞叫着，
星星之火在山丘和平原上闪烁；
黄色、红色和紫色渲染的天空——
日光这样渐逝。

（乔治·库柏）

LESSON 39

I WILL THINK OF IT

我要想一想

chandelier	*Pisa*	*London*	*Ferguson*
portraits	*Isaac*	*invention*	*Galileo*
pendulum	*engine*	*whalebone*	*lectures*
locomotive	*motto*	*England*	*teakettle*
discovered	*swaying*	*discouraged*	*improved*

1. "I will think of it." It is easy to say this; but do you know what great things have come from thinking?

2. We can not see our thoughts, or hear, or taste, or feel them; and yet what mighty power they have!

3. Sir Isaac Newton was seated in his garden on a summer's evening, when he saw an apple fall from a tree. He began to *think*, and, in trying to find out why the apple fell,

discovered how the earth, sun, moon, and stars are kept in their places.

4. A boy named James Watt sat quietly by the fireside, watching the lid of the tea kettle as it moved up and down. He began to *think*; he wanted to find out why the steam in the kettle moved the heavy lid.

5. From that time he went on thinking and thinking; and when he became a man, he improved the steam engine so much that it could, with the greatest ease, do the work of many horses.

6. When you see a steamboat, a steam mill, or a locomotive, remember that it would never have been built if it had not been for the hard thinking of some one.

7. A man named Galileo was once standing in the cathedral of Pisa, when he saw a chandelier swaying to and fro.

8. This set him thinking, and it led to the invention of the pendulum.

9. James Ferguson was a poor Scotch shepherd boy. Once, seeing the inside of a watch, he was filled with wonder. "Why should I not make a watch?" thought he.

10. But how was he to get the materials out of which to make the wheels and the mainspring? He soon found how to get them: he made the mainspring out of a piece of whalebone. He then made a wooden clock which kept good time.

11. He began, also, to copy pictures with a pen, and portraits with oil colors. In a few years, while still a small boy, he earned money enough to support his father.

12. When he became a man, he went to London to live. Some of the wisest men in England, and the king himself, used to attend his lectures. His motto was, "I will think of it;" and he made his thoughts useful to himself and the world.

13. Boys, when you have a difficult lesson to learn, don't feel discouraged, and ask some one to help you before helping yourselves. Think, and by thinking you will learn how to think to some purpose.

【中文阅读】

1. "我要想一想。"这话说起来容易；但是，你知道有多少伟大的事物都来源于思考吗？

2. 我们既看不到思维，也听不到、尝不到、感受不到它；但它却有着多么强大的力量呀！

3. 艾萨克·牛顿先生正是在夏日的一个傍晚，静坐于树下时看到了苹果从树上掉下来。他开始思考，试图找出苹果掉落的原因，从此他竟然发现了地球、太阳、月亮和星星如何维持自己的位置。

4. 一个叫詹姆斯·瓦特的男孩子在炉边静坐时，观察着茶壶盖上上下下地活动。他也陷入了沉思之中，希望能发现壶里的蒸气为什么能够移动沉重的壶盖。

5. 从那时起，他就一直在思考；当他长大成人后，很快就改进了蒸汽机，使它能够轻松地代替马匹工作。

6. 当你看到一艘汽船、一个蒸汽磨或一个火车头时，要记得如果没有某个人的努力思索，它们永远都不会出现。

7. 一个名叫伽利略的人，曾经在比萨教堂前看到一只吊灯晃来晃去。

8. 这让他陷入了思考之中，从而导致了钟摆的发明。

9. 詹姆斯·弗格森曾经是一个贫穷的苏格兰牧童。有一次，他看到了手表的内部构造，心中充满了惊奇。"我为什么不能自己制造一只手表呢？"他想到。

10. 但是，如何才能得到制作轮子和主发条的必要材料呢？很快，他找到了获取材料的方法。他用一根鲸须制成了主发条，然后他做成了一个木制时钟，运转情况一直良好。

11. 同时，他还会用钢笔绘制图片，用油彩临摹肖像。尽管依然还是个小孩子，可这几年中，他挣的钱足以维持自己和父亲的生活了。

12. 长大后，他来到伦敦生活。英国的一些聪明人士经常聆听他的演讲，甚至连国王也是他的忠实听众。他的座右铭就是"我要想一想"，而且他的思想不仅有利于自我，甚至还有利于全世界。

13. 孩子们，当你面对难题时，千万不要气馁，而且在寻求外来帮助之前，应该自己先想想办法。要多思考，通过思索，你将学会如何想要达到某个目的。

LESSON 40

CHARLIE AND ROB

◇

查理和罗伯

1. "Don't you hate splitting wood?" asked Charlie, as he sat down on a log to hinder[1] Rob for a while.

2. "No, I rather like it. When I get hold of a tough old fellow, I say, 'See here, now, you think you're the stronger, and are going to beat me; so I'll split you up into kindling wood.'"

3. "Pshaw!" said Charlie, laughing; "and it's only a stick of wood."

4. "Yes; but you see I pretend it's a lesson, or a tough job of any kind, and it's nice to conquer[2] it."

5. "I don't want to conquer such things; I don't care what becomes of them. I wish I were a man, and a rich one."

6. "Well, Charlie, if you live long enough you'll be a man, without wishing for it; and as for the rich part, I mean to be that myself."

7. "You do. How do you expect to get your money? By sawing wood?"

8. "May be—some of it; that's as good a way as any, so long as it lasts. I don't care how I get rich, you know, so that it's in an honest and useful way."

9. "I'd like to sleep over the next ten years, and wake up to find myself a young man with a splendid[3] education[4] and plenty of money."

10. "Humph! I am not sleepy—a night at a time is enough for me. I mean to work the next ten years. You see there are things that you've got to work out—you can't sleep them out."

11. "I hate work," said Charlie, "that is, such work as sawing and

---

1 Hinder, *interrupt, prevent from working.*

2 Conquer, *overcome, master.*

3 Splendid, *very fine, complete.*

4 Education, *acquired knowledge.*

splitting wood, and doing chores[1]. I'd like to do some big work, like being a clerk in a bank or something of that sort."

12. "Wood has to be sawed and split before it can be burned," said Rob. "I don't know but I'll be a clerk in a bank some time; I'm working towards it. I'm keeping father's accounts for him."

13. How Charlie laughed! "I should think that was a long way from being a bank clerk. I suppose your father sells two tables and six chairs, some days, doesn't he?"

14. "Sometimes more than that, and sometimes not so much," said Rob, in perfect good humor.

15. "I didn't say I was a bank clerk now. I said I was working towards it. Am I not nearer it by keeping a little bit of a book than I should be if I didn't keep any book at all?"

16. "Not a whit—such things happen," said Charlie, as he started to go.

17. Now, which of these boys, do you think, grew up to be a rich and useful

---

1 Chores, *the light work about a house or yard.*

man, and which of them joined a party of tramps before he was thirty years old?

【中文阅读】

1. "你不是讨厌劈木头吗？"查理一边说着，一边坐在一根木头上，不让罗伯继续干下去。

2. "不，我其实很喜欢。当我抓住一根难劈的木头时，我会说，'现在，看这里，你认为自己很强壮，想要打击我，是吗？可是我会把你劈成几半，成为细小的木柴。'"

3. "哼！"查理笑着说，"它不过是一根木头而已。"

4. "是的，但是你看，我把它当成一堂课，或者一份艰苦的工作，这样就很容易战胜它了。"

5. "我并不想征服这样的东西；我不关心这些事情。我只想自己是一个男人，是一个富翁。"

6. "好吧，查理，如果你能活到那时，自然就会成为一个男人，无须多想；至于富翁嘛，我自己也想成为富翁。"

7. "你也想。你怎么挣到钱呀？只靠劈木头？"

8. "也许——有一点吧；只要能够坚持下去，这也是一条不错的路。你知道吗，我并不在乎能够变得多么富有，但是一定要通过正直而有用的途径获得财富。"

9. "我倒希望能好好睡上十年，醒来后发现自己已经成了一个既有教养又有财富的年轻人。"

10. "哼！我不会这样睡过去的——一天只睡一夜，对我来说就足够了。我还要工作十年呢。你看，那里还有很多事情等着你去做呢，睡觉可不能帮你完成它们。"

11. "我讨厌工作，"查理说，"讨厌这些砍柴、劈木头之类的杂活。我想干一番大事业，想当一个银行里的职员，或者类似的工作。"

12. "木头只有被锯掉、被劈碎，才能用来燃烧呀，"罗伯说，"我不知道别的，但是有时候我就像银行里的职员一样，我一直在做这样的工作。我一直在帮爸爸记账呢。"

13. 查理大笑起来！"我想，当一个银行职员还早着呢，我猜想，你的父亲这几天卖掉了两张桌子、六把椅子，是吗？"

14. "有时会更多些，有时还卖不到这么多。"罗伯也不失幽默地附和着。

15. "我并不是说自己现在就是一个银行职员。我是说自己正朝着那个目标努力。通过平常记录小账，不就是朝着这个目标更近了嘛，这难道不比什么也不做更好吗？"

16. "这样的事情根本不会发生。"查理说着便起身准备走了。

17. 现在，你来想想，这两个男孩子中，谁将来长大后会成为富翁，成为一个有用之才；谁又会成为一个三十岁时还流浪街头的人？

LESSON 41

RAY AND HIS KITE

———◇———

芮和他的风筝

1. Ray was thought to be an odd boy. You will think him so, too, when you have read this story.

2. Ray liked well enough to play with the boys at school; yet he liked better to be alone under the shade of some tree, reading a fairy tale or dreaming daydreams[1]. But there was one sport that he liked as well as his companions[2]; that was kiteflying.

3. One day when he was flying his kite, he said to himself, "I wonder if anybody ever tried to fly a kite at night. It seems to me it would be nice. But then, if it were very dark, the kite could not be seen. What if I should fasten a light to it, though? That would make it show. I'll try it this very night."

4. As soon as it was dark, without saying a word to anybody, he took his kite and lantern, and went to a large, open lot, about a quarter of a mile from his home. "Well," thought he, "this is queer. How lonely and still it seems without any other boys around! But I am going to fly my kite, anyway."

5. So he tied the lantern, which was made of tin punched full of small holes, to the tail of his kite. Then he pitched the kite, and, after several attempts[3], succeeded in making it rise. Up it went, higher and higher, as Ray let out the string. When the string was all unwound, he tied it to a fence; and then he stood and gazed at his kite as it floated high up in the air.

6. While Ray was enjoying his sport, some people who were out on

---

1 Daydreams, *vain fancies*.

2 Companions, *playmates. friends*.

3 Attempts, *trials, efforts*.

the street in the village, saw a strange light in the sky. They gathered in groups[1] to watch it. Now it was still for a few seconds, then it seemed to be

jumping up and down; then it made long sweeps[2] back and forth through the air.

7. "What can it be?" said one person. "How strange!" said another. "It can not be a comet[3]; for comets have tails," said a third. "Perhaps it's a big firefly," said another.

8. At last some of the men determined[4] to find out what this strange light was— whether it was a hobgoblin[5] dancing in the air, or something dropped from the sky. So off they started to get as near it as they could.

9. While this was taking place, Ray, who had got tired of standing, was seated in a fence corner, behind a tree. He could see the men as they approached; but they did not see him.

---

1 Groups, *several together, small assemblages.*

2 Sweeps, *rapid movements in the line of a curve.*

3 Comet, *a brilliant heavenly body with a long, fiery tail.*

4 Determined, *concluded, resolved.*

5 Hobgoblin, *an ugly fairy or imp.*

10. When they were directly under the light, and saw what it was, they looked at each other, laughing, and said, "This is some boy's trick; and it has fooled us nicely. Let us keep the secret, and have our share of the joke."

11. Then they laughed again, and went back to the village; and some of the simple people there have not yet found out what that strange light was.

12. When the men had gone, Ray thought it was time for him to go; so he wound up his string, picked up his kite and lantern, and went home. His mother had been wondering what had become of him.

13. When she heard what he had been doing, she hardly knew whether to laugh or scold; but I think she laughed, and told him that it was time for him to go to bed.

【中文阅读】

1. 芮被公认为是一个奇怪的小男孩。当你看到这个故事时，也会这么认为的。

2. 芮很喜欢和其他的男孩子在学校里玩耍；但是，他更喜欢独自坐在树下的阴凉处，看神话故事或者做白日梦。不过，有一项体育活动让他和其他的小伙伴一样着迷，那就是放风筝。

3. 有一天，当他正在放风筝时，自言自语地说："我很奇怪，有人在晚上放风筝吗。在我看来，这样做可能很有趣。但是，如果天特别黑的话，又怎么能看到风筝呢。如果我在风筝上加一盏灯，又会怎样呢？这样就能让人看到它了。我想在今天晚上试一试。"

4. 等天黑下来后，他对谁也没有说，径自拿着风筝和灯笼来到了一片开阔、空旷的地里，那里离他家只有四分之一英里远。他心里想："好吧，这样做的确有点奇怪。周围没有其他小朋友，看上去是很孤独和寂寞！但是，无论如何，我要开始放飞自己的风筝了。"

5. 于是，他把一个满是小孔的锡制灯笼系在风筝的尾巴上。接着，他掷出了风筝，经过几次努力，他才成功地使风筝升起来。芮松开了线绳，风筝不断地上升，越来越高。当所有的线绳都被松开后，他将风筝线绑在一个栅栏上，然后站在那里盯着自己的风筝看，而那风筝就在空中飘浮着。

6. 就在芮正享受着自己的游戏时，村子里一些在街上行走的人看见了空中奇怪的灯光。他们聚集到一起，抬头望着天空。这才刚刚放飞了几秒钟，它好像还在上下乱窜，一会儿又开始前前后后地飘忽不定。

7. "那是什么东西呀？"其中一个人说。"多么奇怪呀！"另一个人说。"它不可能是彗星，因为彗星都有长长的尾巴，"第三个人说。"或许，它是一只大萤火虫。"又传来另外一个人的声音。

8. 最后，其中几个人决定要去探个究竟，到底这个灯光是什么怪物——到底是妖怪在空中乱舞呢，还是从天上掉下来的什么东西。于是，他们开始尽可能地慢慢靠近那个灯光。

9. 就在人们猜测时，一直站在那里的芮感到有些疲惫，便在栅栏旁的角落里坐了下来，背靠着一棵大树。当那些人慢慢走过来时，他能看到了人们，但是人们却看不到他。

10. 当人们径直走到灯光下，看清楚了它的本来面目时，互相看看，都笑了起来，有人说："这不过是孩子们的鬼把戏；却愚弄了我们。大家都保守这个秘密，和他们一起开这个玩笑吧。"

11. 然后，他们又笑了起来，纷纷走回村子里；有一些头脑简单的人却还没有发现这个奇怪的光到底是什么东西。

12. 人们离开后，芮也觉着是时候该回家了；于是，他收紧了风筝线，捡起风筝和灯笼回家了。妈妈也正在纳闷，他究竟去干什么了。

13. 当她听完芮的描述，都不知道应该笑他还是该骂他了；但是，我认为她笑了，而且还会告诉芮应该去睡觉了。

LESSON 42
BEWARE OF THE FIRST DRINK

◇

谨防第一次饮酒

1. "Uncle Philip, as the day is fine, will you take a walk with us this morning?"

2. "Yes, boys. Let me get my hat and cane, and we will take a ramble. I will tell you a story as we go. Do you know poor old Tom Smith?"

3. "Know him! Why, Uncle Philip, everybody knows him. He is such a shocking drunkard, and swears so horribly[1]."

4. "Well, I have known him ever since we were boys together. There was not a more decent[2], well-behaved boy among us. After he left school, his father died, and he was put into a store in the city. There, he fell into bad company.

5. "Instead of spending his evenings in reading, he would go to the theater and to balls. He soon learned to play cards, and of course to play for money. He lost more than he could pay.

6. "He wrote to his poor mother, and told her his losses. She sent him money to pay his debts, and told him to come home.

7. "He did come home. After all, he might still have been useful and happy, for his friends were willing to forgive the past. For a time, things went on well. He married a lovely woman, gave up his bad habits, and was doing well.

8. "But one thing, boys, ruined him forever. In the city, he had learned to take strong drink, and he said to me once, that when a man begins to drink, he never knows where it will end. 'Therefore,' said Tom, 'beware of the first drink!'

9. "It was not long before he began to follow his old habit. He knew the danger, but it seemed as if he could not resist[3] his desire to drink. His poor mother soon died of grief and shame. His lovely wife followed her to the grave.

---

1 Horribly, *in a dreadful manner, terribly.*

2 Decent, *modest, respectable.*

3 Resist, *withstand, overcome.*

10. "He lost the respect of all, went on from bad to worse, and has long been a perfect sot[1]. Last night, I had a letter from the city, stating that Tom Smith had been found guilty[2] of stealing, and sent to the state prison for ten years.

11. "There I suppose he will die, for he is now old. It is dreadful to think to what an end he has come. I could not but think, as I read the letter, of what he said to me years ago, 'Beware of the first drink!'

12. "Ah, my dear boys, when old Uncle Philip is gone, remember that he told you the story of Tom Smith, and said to you, 'Beware of the first drink!' The man who does this will never be a drunkard."

【中文阅读】

1."菲利普叔叔，今天天气真好，上午您会和我们一起出去散步吗？"

2."好的，孩子们。我去拿帽子和手杖，然后四处走走，我会在路上给你们讲一个故事。你们认识可怜的老汉，汤姆·史密斯吗？"

---

1 Sot, *an habitual drunkard.*

2 Guilty, *justly chargeable with a crime.*

3. "认识他! 怎么了, 菲利普叔叔, 所有人都认识他呀。他是一个令人厌恶的酒鬼, 而且骂起人来很吓人。"

4. "我可认识他很久了, 因为我们自小就在一起玩耍。我们当中没有一个孩子是乖巧得体的好孩子。离开学校后, 他的父亲去世了, 于是他被送到市里的一家商店。在那里, 他遇到了不好的伙伴。"

5. "他并没有将晚上的业余时间用来读书, 反而去戏院、去打球玩。很快, 他就玩起了扑克牌, 当然是玩钱的那种。他输掉的钱比自己挣到的钱还多。"

6. "他给妈妈写信诉说了自己的损失, 妈妈寄来钱让他还债, 还告诉他尽快回家去。"

7. "他并没有回家。毕竟, 朋友们都愿意原谅他过去的行为, 他或许依然快乐地生活着, 而且还认为自己尚有用武之地。有一段时间, 事情进展得很顺利。他娶了一个可爱的女人, 也戒除了自己的恶习, 日子过得很好。"

8. "孩子们, 但是有一件事却毁了他一生。在城市里, 他学会了喝烈酒, 他曾经对我说过, 当一个男人开始酗酒, 就永无终结了。汤姆说过'因此, 千万要谨慎对待自己的第一次喝酒!'"

9. "就在不久前, 他的老毛病又犯了。他自己也知道这样很危险, 但是似乎无法抗拒想要喝酒的欲望。他那可怜的妈妈很快就因过度悲痛和羞愧而过世了。他的爱妻也追随母亲离去。"

10. "他失去了尊严, 情况越来越糟糕, 完全成了一个不折不扣的醉鬼。昨天晚上, 我收到了市里寄来的一封信. 提到汤姆·史密斯因盗窃罪而被送进州监狱服刑十年。"

11. "我猜他可能会死在监狱里, 因为他现在已经老了。我甚至都不敢去想他的末日会是什么样子, 非常可怕。当我读到这封信时, 禁不住想起几年前他对我说的话, '要当心第一次喝酒!'"

12. "啊, 我亲爱的孩子们, 菲利普叔叔走后, 你们要记得他曾经告诉过你们汤姆·史密斯的故事, 并且还对你们说过, '要当心第一次饮酒!'一个谨慎对待饮酒的人永远不会成为一个醉鬼。"

LESSON 43

SPEAK GENTLY

◆

请轻声说话

1. Speak gently; it is better far
     To rule by love than fear:
   Speak gently; let no harsh words mar[1]
     The good we might do here.

2. Speak gently to the little child;
     Its love be sure to gain;
   Teach it in accents[2] soft and mild;
     It may not long remain.

3. Speak gently to the aged one;
     Grieve not the careworn heart:
   The sands of life are nearly run;
     Let such in peace depart.

4. Speak gently, kindly, to the poor;
     Let no harsh tone be heard;
   They have enough they must endure[3],
     Without an unkind word.

---

1 Mar, *injure, hurt.*
2 Accents, *language, tones.*
3 Endure, *bear, suffer.*

5. Speak gently to the erring[1]; know
   They must have toiled in vain;
Perhaps unkindness made them so;
   Oh, win them back again.

6. Speak gently: 't is a little thing
   Dropped in the heart's deep well;
The good, the joy, which it may bring,
   Eternity[2] shall tell.

(*George Washington Langford*)

【中文阅读】

1. 请轻声说话,
   爱的力量胜于恐惧的统治;
   请轻声说话,
   勿让刺耳之语成为美德的瑕疵。

2. 请对小朋友轻声说话,
   无疑你将得到他们的爱;
   教导的音调宜温柔文雅,
   否则爱就不再存留。

3. 请对长者轻声说话,
   饱经忧患的心不应再感悲伤;
   生命的沙漏即将停下,
   让他们平静离场。

---

1 Erring, *sinning*.
2 Eternity, *the endless hereafter, the future*.

4. 请对穷苦之人轻声和蔼说话，
   不让他们听到严苛的音调；
   他们忍受的苦难已够巨大，
   即使一个刻薄的字眼也不曾听到。
   即使没有无情的话语，
   他们要忍受的苦难也已够多。

5. 请向做过错事的人轻声说话，
   要知道他们必定经历过徒劳的挣扎；
   也许就是无情的对待让他们把过错犯下，
   噢，把他们再争取回来吧。

6. 请轻声说话，
   这微不足道却能深入人心，
   它可能激发美德，创造欢乐，
   直到永恒不竭不尽。

（乔治·华盛顿·兰福德）

LESSON 44

THE SEVEN STICKS

◇

七根棍子

1. A man had seven sons, who were always quarreling. They left their studies and work, to quarrel among themselves. Some bad men were looking forward to the death of their father, to cheat[1] them out of their property[2] by making them quarrel about it.

2. The good old man, one day, called his sons around him. He laid before them seven sticks, which were bound together. He said, "I will pay a hundred dollars to the one who can break this bundle[3]."

3. Each one strained every nerve[4] to break the bundle. After a long but vain trial, they all said that it could not be done.

---

1 Cheat, *deceive, wrong.*

2 Property, *that which one owns—whether land, goods, or money.*

3 Bundle, *a number of things bound together.*

4 Nerve, *sinew, muscle.*

4. "And yet, my boys," said the father, "nothing is easier to do." He then untied the bundle, and broke the sticks, one by one, with perfect ease.

5. "Ah!" said his sons, "it is easy enough to do it so; anybody could do it in that way."

6. Their father replied, "As it is with these sticks, so is it with you, my sons. So long as you hold fast together and aid each other, you will prosper[1], and none can injure you.

7. "But if the bond of union[2] be broken, it will happen to you just as it has to these sticks, which lie here broken on the ground."

> Home, city, country, all are prosperous found,
> When by the powerful link of union bound.

【中文阅读】

1. 有一个人，他有七个爱吵架的儿子。他们不顾学习和工作，互相吵个不停。有些坏人等着他们父亲的死期到来，挑拨他们为家产而争吵，到时好趁机骗取他们的财产。

2. 有一天，善良的老人把儿子们都召集到身边，把绑在一起的七根棍子放在他们面前，说："谁能把这一捆棍子折断，我就给他一百美元。"

3. 每个人都使出了九牛二虎之力，花了很长时间还是徒劳无功。他们都说，要折断这些棍子根本办不到。

4. "其实不然，我的孩子们，"父亲说道，"没有比这更容易做到的事情了。"说完他解开了绳子，毫不费劲地就把那七根棍子一根一根地折断了。

5. "啊！"儿子们说，"这么做太容易了。用这种方式，任何人都做得到。"

6. 他们的父亲回答道："你们七兄弟就像这些棍子一样，我的孩子们。只要你们紧密地团结在一起，互相帮助，你们就会取得成功，谁也不能伤害你们。"

7. "但是，一旦打破了这种团结，你们就会像这些棍子一样，一根一根地被折断在地上。"

家庭、城市、国家，无不是由各个部分强有力地连结而成的联合体，只有团结一致，才能兴盛发展。

---

1 Prosper, *succeed, do well.*

2 Union, *the state of being joined or united.*

LESSON 45

THE MOUNTAIN SISTER

◇

山妹子

1. The home of little Jeannette is far away, high up among the mountains. Let us call her our mountain sister.

2. There are many things you would like to hear about her, but I can only tell you now how she goes with her father and brother, in the autumn, to help gather nuts for the long winter.

3. A little way down the mountain side is a chestnut[1] wood. Did you ever see a chestnut tree? In the spring its branches are covered with bunches of creamy flowers, like long tassels[2]. All the hot summer these are turning into sweet nuts, wrapped[3] safely in large, prickly[4], green balls.

4. But when the frost

---

1 Chestnut, *a tree valuable for its timber and its fruit.*

2 Tassels, *hanging ornaments, such as are used on curtains.*

3 Wrapped, *completely covered up, inclosed.*

4 Prickly, *covered with sharp points.*

of autumn comes, these prickly balls turn brown, and crack open. Then you may see inside one, two, three, and even four, sweet, brown nuts.

5. When her father says, one night at supper time, "I think there will be a frost tonight," Jeannette knows very well what to do. She dances away early in the evening to her little bed, made in a box built up against the wall.

6. Soon she falls asleep to dream about the chestnut wood, and the little brook that springs from rock to rock down under the tall, dark trees. She wakes with the first daylight, and is out of bed in a minute, when she hears her father's cheerful call, "Come, children; it is time to be off."

7. Their dinner is ready in a large basket. The donkey stands before the door with great bags for the nuts hanging at each side. They go merrily over the crisp[1], white frost to the chestnut trees. How the frost has opened

1 Crisp, *brittle, sparkling*.

the burs[1]! It has done half their work for them already.

8. How they laugh and sing, and shout to each other as they fill their baskets! The sun looks down through the yellow leaves; the rocks give them mossy seats; the birds and squirrels wonder what these strange people are doing in their woods.

9. Jeannette really helps, though she is only a little girl; and her father says at night, that his Jane is a dear, good child. This makes her very happy. She thinks about it at night, when she says her prayers. Then she goes to sleep to dream of the merry autumn days.

10. Such is our little mountain sister, and here is a picture of her far-away home. The mountain life is ever a fresh and happy one.

【中文阅读】

1. 小珍妮特的家很远，在大山里高高的地方，我们就叫她山妹子吧！

2. 关于她的许多故事你一定很想听，可是在这里我只告诉你，她帮着父亲和哥哥在秋天里采集栗子以备长冬之用的情形。

3. 往山下走一点点路，是一片栗子林。你是否见过栗子树呢？春天里，栗子树的枝干被奶油一样的花朵密密麻麻地覆盖着，像长长的流苏。夏天，这些花儿会变成甜美的板栗，完好无损地包裹在多刺的绿色大球球里。

4. 到了秋天雾起的时候，这些带刺的球球就变成褐色，爆裂开来，这时你会看见里面有一个、两个、三个，甚至四个褐色的甜栗子。

5. 有一天，晚饭时分，珍妮特的父亲说："我想今天晚上会起雾。"珍妮特很清楚地知道将要做什么。当天晚上，她轻快地跳着舞步回到自己的小床边。

6. 很快她就沉入了梦乡，梦见栗子树林，还有林间的小溪，在高大而浓密的树林间，漫流在岩石上。伴随着第一缕晨光醒来，她马上起床，就听到父亲高兴地呼唤："来吧，孩子们，是时候出发了。"

7. 他们的午餐已经备好，放在一个大篮子里。驴子已经站立在门前等候，两侧驮着用来装栗子的大袋子。他们轻快地踏过易脆的白霜，向栗子林进发。秋霜把刺果打开了那么多！已经帮他们干了一半的活儿。

---

1 Burs, *the rough coverings of seeds or nuts.*

8. 他们又笑又唱，一边互相喊话，一边把栗子往袋子里装，多么快乐啊！太阳穿过金黄的叶子之间俯视着他们；岩石为他们准备好铺满青苔的座位；小鸟和松鼠好奇地看着他们，不知道这些奇怪的人在它们的树林里做什么。

9. 虽然珍妮特只是一个小姑娘，但却是个好帮手；晚上她的父亲说，小珍是个让人疼爱的乖孩子。这让她很高兴。晚上祈祷的时候，她想到了这些，然后上床睡觉，做起了愉快的秋天之梦。

10. 这就是我们的山妹子，这就是她那遥远的家的一个画面。山里的生活永远是新鲜而快乐的。

LESSON 46

HARRY AND THE GUIDEPOST

---◇---

哈里和路牌

1. The night was dark, the sun was hid
   Beneath the mountain gray,
   And not a single star appeared
   To shoot a silver ray.

2. Across the heath[1] the owlet flew,
   And screamed along the blast;
   And onward, with a quickened step,
   Benighted[2] Harry passed.

3. Now, in thickest darkness plunged,
   He groped[3] his way to find;
   And now, he thought he saw beyond,
   A form of horrid[4] kind.

4. In deadly white it upward rose,
   Of cloak and mantle bare,
   And held its naked arms across,
   To catch him by the hair.

5. Poor Harry felt his blood run cold,

---

1 Heath, *a place overgrown with shrubs.*
2 Benighted, *overtaken by the night.*
3 Groped, *felt his way in the dark.*
4 Horrid, *hideous, frightful.*

At what before him stood;
But then, thought he, no harm, I'm sure,
Can happen to the good.

6. So, calling all his courage up,
   He to the monster[1] went;
   And eager through the dismal[2] gloom
   His piercing[3] eyes he bent.

7. And when he came well nigh the ghost[4]
   That gave him such affright,
   He clapped his hands upon his side,
   And loudly laughed outright.

8. For 't was a friendly guidepost[5] stood,
   His wandering steps to guide;
   And thus he found that to the good,
   No evil could betide[6].

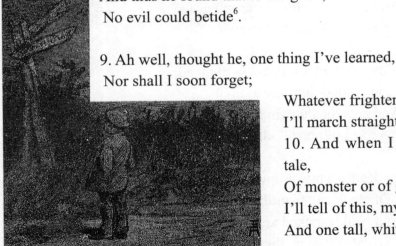

9. Ah well, thought he, one thing I've learned,
   Nor shall I soon forget;
   Whatever frightens me again,
   I'll march straight up to it.
10. And when I hear an idle[7]
    tale,
    Of monster or of ghost,
    I'll tell of this, my lonely walk,
    And one tall, white guidepost.

---

1 Monster, *a thing of unnatural size and shape.*
2 Dismal, *dark, cheerless.*
3 Piercing, *sharp, penetrating.*
4 Ghost, *a frightful object in white, an apparition.*
5 Guidepost, *a post and sign set up at the forks of a road to directed travelers.*
6 Betide, *befall, happen.*
7 Idle, *of no account, foolish.*

136

【中文阅读】

1. 夜色漆黑一片，
   太阳隐藏在灰暗的山后；
   天上看不到一颗星，
   不见一丝银光。

2. 猫头鹰飞过荒野，
   一阵尖叫声掠过；
   加快脚步向前冲，
   哈里的身后已被夜色包围。

3. 此时，陷入最深沉的黑暗
   他摸索着探寻前路；
   此刻，他觉得自己看见
   远处一个可怕的怪物。

4. 死寂般苍白怪物向上立起，
   没穿披风斗篷的它光溜溜，
   交叉着赤裸的双臂，
   似要抓住哈里的头发使劲揪。

5. 看到眼前站立的这个东西
   可怜的哈里感到毛骨悚然；
   他转念一想，我相信，
   好人一生平安。

6. 他鼓起全部勇气，
   迎面走向怪物；
   热切渴望穿过阴沉的黑暗，
   他那似要刺穿一切的双眼无比专注。

7. 当怪物近在咫尺，
　　那个令他如此恐惧的幽灵，
　　他不禁扬起手拍在它身上，
　　失声大笑不停。

8. 站在面前的是友善的路牌，
　　为指引他流浪的脚步；
　　这更让他彻底明白，
　　邪灵无法阻挡好人的路。

9. 啊，好吧，他想，
　　我上了一课，我将好好记住；
　　无论何事让我恐慌，
　　我将踏着大步直面而上。

10. 当我听到愚蠢的故事，
　　说有幽灵或鬼怪，
　　我会讲述这次寂寞夜路的经历，
　　还有那高高的白色路牌。

LESSON 47

THE MONEY AMY DID NOT EARN

◇

艾米没有赚到的钱

1. Amy was a dear little girl, but she was too apt to waste time in getting ready to do her tasks[1], instead of doing them at once as she ought.

2. In the village in which she lived, Mr. Thornton kept a store where he sold fruit of all kinds, including berries in their season[2]. One day he said to Amy, whose parents were quite poor, "Would you like to earn some money?"

3. "Oh, yes," replied she, "for I want some new shoes, and papa has no money to buy them with."

4. "Well, Amy," said Mr. Thornton, "I noticed some fine, ripe blackberries in Mr. Green's pasture to-day, and he said that anybody was welcome to them. I will pay you thirteen cents a quart[3] for all you will pick for me."

5. Amy was delighted at the thought of earning some money; so she ran home to get a basket, intending to go immediately to pick the berries.

6. Then she thought she would like to know how much money she would get if she picked five quarts. With the help of her slate and pencil, she found out that she would get sixty-five cents.

7. "But supposing I should pick a dozen quarts," thought she, "how much should I earn then?" "Dear me," she said, after figuring[4] a while, "I should earn a dollar and fifty-six cents."

8. Amy then found out what Mr. Thornton would pay her for fifty,

---

1 Tasks, *work which one has to do.*

2 Season, *proper time of the year.*

3 Quart, *the fourth part of a gallon.*

4 Figuring, *computing, calculating.*

a hundred, and two hundred quarts. It took her some time to do this, and then it was so near dinner time that she had to stay at home until afternoon.

9. As soon as dinner was over, she took her basket and hurried[1] to the pasture. Some boys had been there before dinner, and all the ripe berries were picked. She could not find enough to fill a quart measure[2].

10. As Amy went home, she thought of what her teacher had often told her—"Do your task at once; then think about it," for "one doer is worth a hundred dreamers."

---

1 Hurried, *went rapidly*.

2 Measure, *vessel*.

【中文阅读】

1. 艾米是个可爱的小姑娘，可是她太容易把时间浪费在准备做事的过程中，而不是有应该做的事情就马上去做。

2. 在她住的村子里，桑顿先生开了一家店，店里出售各种各样的水果，包括各个时令的浆果。有一天他对父母穷困的艾米说："你想不想赚一些钱？"

3. "噢，想的，"她回答说，"因为我想买双新鞋子，可是爸爸没有钱给我买。"

4. "那好，艾米，"桑顿先生说，"今天我看到格林先生的牧场里有些漂亮的黑莓成熟了，他说欢迎任何人云采摘。你去帮我摘回来，每一夸脱我将付给你一角三分钱。"

5. 想到可以赚钱，艾米很高兴。于是她跑回家去拿篮子，打算立即就去采摘黑莓。

6. 然后，她想知道如果她能采摘到五夸脱黑莓的话，将会赚到多少钱。用铅笔在石板上算了一阵，她算出来那将会是六角五分。

7. "可要是我能摘到12夸脱呢，"她又想，"那我又该赚到多少钱呢？""哎呀，"算了一会儿以后，她说，"我将会赚到一美元五角六分。"

8. 接着艾米又算出了如果她采摘到50夸脱、100夸脱甚至200夸脱黑莓的话，桑顿先生分别该付给她多少钱。这花掉了她不少的时间，这时已经快到午饭时间了，所以她不得不留在家里，直到下午。

9. 吃完午饭，艾米拿起篮子，急忙到牧场去。有些男孩子午饭前就已经在那里了，所有成熟了的黑莓都被摘走了。她能找到的还不够一夸脱的分量。

10. 在回家的路上，艾米想起了老师经常对她说的话——"立刻去做应该做的事，然后再去思考，"因为，"一个实干者抵得上一百个梦想家。"

LESSON 48
WHO MADE THE STARS

◇

星星是谁造的

1. "Mother, who made the stars, which light
   The beautiful blue sky?
   Who made the moon, so clear and bright,
   That rises up so high?"

2. "'T was God, my child, the Glorious[1] One,
   He formed them by his power;
   He made alike the brilliant sun,
   And every leaf and flower.

3. "He made your little feet to walk;
   Your sparkling eyes to see;
   Your busy, prattling[2] tongue to talk,
   And limbs so light and free.

4. "He paints each fragrant flower that blows[3],
   With loveliness and bloom;
   He gives the violet and the rose
   Their beauty and perfume[4].

---

1 Glorious, *excellent, exalted.*
2 Prattling, *talking lightly like a child.*
3 Blows, *blossoms.*
4 Perfume, *delightful odor.*

5. "Our various[1] wants his hands supply;
   He guides us every hour;
We're kept beneath his watchful eye,
   And guarded by his power.

6. "Then let your little heart, my love,
   Its grateful homage[2] pay
To that kind Friend, who, from above,
   Thus guides you every day.

7. "In all the changing scenes[3] of time,
   On Him our hopes depend;
In every age, in every clime[4],
   Our Father and our Friend."

【中文阅读】

1. 妈妈，星星是谁造的，
   它的光把美丽的蓝色夜空照亮?
   是谁造的月亮，如此清澈，闪耀光芒，
   高高地挂在天上?

2. 那是上帝，我的孩子，荣耀的主，
   他用神力创造了星星月亮;
   同样是他，创造了灿烂的太阳，
   以及所有草叶和花香。

3. 他为你造了小脚丫走天下，

---

1 Various, *many and different.*

2 Homage, *respect.*

3 Scenes, *events.*

4 Clime, *climate, region.*

给你明亮的眼睛看宇宙；
你忙碌的舌头咿呀呀爱说话，
还有四肢轻盈又自由。

4. 他画出每一朵芳香的花，
　　花朵娇美盛放；
　　他赋予紫罗兰和玫瑰花
　　独有的美和芬芳。

5. 他的双手满足我们种种匮乏；
　　他每时每刻引导我们前行；
　　我们永远处于他的关注之下，
　　由他的权能庇护得安宁。

6. 我的爱，让你小小的心灵，
　　把它感恩的崇敬
　　归于那来自天上的仁慈的朋友，
　　让你每天跟从他的引领。

7. 在每个时光变幻的舞台，
　　他都是我们希望的源头；
　　无论何地，在任何时代，
　　我们的天父我们的朋友。

LESSON 49

DEEDS OF KINDNESS

◇

善 举

1. One day, as two little boys were walking along the road, they overtook a woman carrying a large basket of apples.

2. The boys thought the woman looked very pale and tired; so they said, "Are you going to town? If you are, we will carry your basket."

3. "Thank you," replied the woman, "you are very kind: you see I am

weak and ill." Then she told them that she was a widow[1], and had a lame son to support.

4. She lived in a cottage three miles away, and was now going to market to sell the apples which grew on the only tree in her little garden. She wanted the money to pay her rent.

5. "We are going the same way you are," said the boys. "Let us have the basket;" and they took hold of it, one on each side, and trudged[2] along with merry hearts.

6. The poor widow looked glad, and said that she hoped their mother would not be angry with them. "Oh, no," they replied; "our mother has taught us to be kind to everybody, and to be useful in any way that we can."

7. She then offered to give them a few of the ripest apples for their trouble. "No, thank you," said they; "we do not want any pay for what we have done."

8. When the widow got home, she told her lame son what had happened on the road, and they were both made happier that day by the kindness of the two boys.

9. The other day, I saw a little girl stop and pick up a piece of orange peel, which she threw into the gutter[3]. "I wish the boys would not throw orange peel on the sidewalk," said she. "Some one may tread[4] upon it, and fall."

10. "That is right, my dear," I said. "It is a little thing for you to do what you have done, but it shows that you have a thoughtful mind and a feeling heart."

11. Perhaps some may say that these are little things. So they are; but we must not wait for occasions[5] to do great things. We must begin with little labors of love.

---

1 Widow, *a woman whose husband is dead.*
2 Trudged, *walked.*
3 Gutter, *the lower ground or channel along the side of a road.*
4 Tread, *step.*
5 Occasions, *chances, opportunities.*

【中文阅读】

1. 有一天，两个小男孩走在路上的时候，遇上了一个提着一大篮子苹果的妇人。

2. 两个男孩觉得妇人看起来苍白而疲倦，于是问道："您是要进城吗？如果是的话，我们来帮你提着篮子。"

3. "谢谢你们，"妇人回答，"你们真好，看我虚弱生病而帮助我。"接着她告诉他们，她是个寡妇，抚养着一个瘸腿的儿子。

4. 她住在三英里外的一座小农舍里，现在是要到集市上，把从自家院子里唯一的树上摘下来的苹果卖掉。她需要钱交房租。

5. "我们与您同路，"男孩说，"让我们提着篮子吧。"然后他们把篮子接了过来，一人一边抬着走，步履艰难，心情却很愉快。

6. 可怜的寡妇看上去很高兴，说她希望他们的母亲不会为此生他们的气。"噢，不会的，"他们回答，"妈妈教我们要友好对待所有人，并且尽力做有用之人。"

7. 接着妇人提出要给他们几个最红的苹果，作为麻烦他们的酬劳。"不，谢谢您，"他们说，"我们做这些事情不需要任何报酬。"

8. 寡妇回到家里以后，把路上发生的事情告诉了跛脚的儿子。那一天他们俩都因为两个男孩的善举而更加快乐。

9. 第二天，我见到一个小姑娘停下来，捡起一块橙皮，把它丢到了沟里。"我希望那些男孩不要把果皮扔在人行道上，"她说，"会有人踩到果皮，然后摔倒。"

10. "说得对，亲爱的，"我说，"你刚刚做的事情对你来说只是举手之劳，却体现出你是个体贴人而富有同情心的小姑娘。"

11. 也许有的人会说这些都是小事情。确实是的，然而我们不能干等着做大事的机会。我们得心甘情愿从小事情做起。

LESSON 50

THE ALARM CLOCK

---◇---

闹　钟

1. A lady, who found it not easy to wake in the morning as early as she wished, bought an alarm[1] clock. These clocks are so made as to strike with a loud whirring[2] noise at any hour the owner pleases to set them.

2. The lady placed her clock at the head of the bed, and at the right time she found herself roused[3] by the long, rattling[4] sound.

3. She arose at once, and felt better all day for her early rising. This lasted for some weeks. The alarm clock faithfully[5] did its duty[6], and was plainly heard so long as it was obeyed.

4. But, after a time, the lady grew tired of early rising. When she was waked by the noise, she merely[7] turned over in bed, and slept again.

5. In a few days, the clock ceased to rouse her from her sleep. It spoke just as loudly as ever; but she did not hear it, because she had been in the habit of not obeying it.

6. Finding that she might as well be without it, she resolved that when she heard the sound she would jump up.

7. Just so it is with conscience[8]. If we will obey its voice, even in the most trifling[9] things, we can always hear it, clear and strong.

---

1 Alarm, *a sudden sound calculated to awaken persons from sleep.*
2 Whirring, *buzzing.*
3 Roused, *waked.*
4 Rattling, *giving quick, sharp noises in rapid succession.*
5 Faithfully, *in an exact and proper manner.*
6 Duty, *the right conduct or action.*
7 Merely, *simply.*
8 Conscience, *that within us which tells what is right and what is wrong, reason.*
9 Trifling, *of little importance or value.*

8. But if we allow[1] ourselves to do what we have some fears may not be quite right, we shall grow more and more sleepy, until the voice of conscience has no longer power to wake us.

【中文阅读】

1. 有一位女士，发现不容易像自己希望的那样在清晨早点醒来，于是她买了一个闹钟。闹钟被制造出来，就是为了在主人设定的任何时间发出响亮的声音。

2. 女士把闹钟放在床头，到了设定的准确时间，她发现自己被一阵很长的咔嗒声吵醒了。

3. 她马上起床，一整天都因为早起而感觉更好。这样的情况持续了几个星期。闹钟忠诚地尽职尽责，而且只要主人服从闹钟的指令，就能按时听到它的声音。

4. 然而，过了一段时间以后，这位女士厌倦了早起。被闹钟声吵醒之后，她只是在床上翻一个身，然后继续睡觉。

5. 几天以后，闹钟不再能使她从睡梦中醒来。闹钟声还是一如既往地响亮，但她听而不见，因为她已经习惯了不再听从闹钟的指令。

6. 意识到她这样还不如没有闹钟，女士下定决心，一听到闹钟的声音，就跳起来。

7. 良心也是一样。如果我们愿意听从它的声音，即使是关于最细微的事情，我们也总是能听到，清晰而强劲。

8. 然而，要是我们任由自己去做我们担心不是很正确的一些事情，我们就会变得越来越困，直到良心的声音不再有力量把我们唤醒。

---

1 Allow, *permit, suffer.*

LESSON 51
SPRING

春

1. The alder[1] by the river
   Shakes out her powdery curls;
   The willow buds in silver
   For little boys and girls.

2. The little birds fly over,
   And oh, how sweet they sing!
   To tell the happy children
   That once again't is Spring.

3. The gay green grass comes creeping
   So soft beneath their feet;
   The frogs begin to ripple[2]
   A music clear and sweet.

4. And buttercups are coming,
   And scarlet columbine,
   And in the sunny meadows
   The dandelions shine.

5. And just as many daisies
   As their soft hands can hold,

---

1 Alder, *a tree which grows in moist land.*
2 Ripple, *to cause little waves of sound.*

The little ones may gather,
All fair in white and gold.

6. Here blows the warm red clover,
   There peeps the violet blue;
   Oh, happy little children!
   God made them all for you.

(Celia Thaxter)

【中文阅读】

1. 河岸边的桤木
   抖出粉状的卷；
   柳树萌发银芽
   为了那些孩儿。

2. 小鸟飞过来，
   噢，歌声多美妙！
   它们告诉快乐的小孩，
   春天回来了。

3. 青翠的小草慢慢隆起
   在他们脚下如此柔软，
   青蛙在水里此起彼落，
   如乐音清脆而婉转。

4. 毛茛也蓄势待发

　　还有红色的耧斗菜，

　　在阳光照耀的草地上，

　　蒲公英焕发光彩。

5. 他们柔软的小手能握住多少，

　　遍地的雏菊就有多少，

　　小家伙们可以尽情采摘，

　　雪白和金黄的小花多美好。

6. 这儿有热情的红三叶草迎风点头

　　那边蓝色紫罗兰也含羞亮相，

　　噢，快乐的小孩！

　　上帝是为了你们创造如此春光。

（西莉亚 · 萨克斯特）

LESSON 52

TRUE COURAGE

◇

真正的勇气

One cold winter's day, three boys were passing by a schoolhouse. The oldest was a bad boy, always in trouble himself, and trying to get others into trouble. The youngest, whose name was George, was a very good boy.

George wished to do right, but was very much wanting in courage. The other boys were named Henry and James. As they walked along, they talked as follows:

Henry. What fun it would be to throw a snowball against the schoolroom door, and make the teacher and scholars[1] all jump!

James. You would jump, if you should. If the teacher did not catch you and whip you, he would tell your father, and you would get a whipping[2] then; and that would make you jump higher than the scholars, I think.

Henry. Why, we would get so far off, before the teacher could come to the door, that he could not tell who we are. Here is a snowball just as hard as ice, and George would as soon throw it against the door as not.

James. Give it to him, and see He would not dare[3] to throw it.

Henry. Do you think George is a coward? You do not know him as well as I do. Here, George, take this snowball, and show James that you are not such a coward as he thinks you are.

George. I am not afraid to throw it; but I do not want to. I do not see that it will do any good, or that there will be any fun in it.

James. There! I told you he would not dare to throw it.

---

1 Scholars, *children at school.*

2 Whipping, *punishment.*

3 Dare, *have courage.*

Henry. Why, George, are you turning coward? I thought you did not fear anything. Come, save your credit[1], and throw it. I know you are not afraid.

George. Well, I am not afraid to throw. Give me the snowball. I would as soon throw it as not.

Whack! went the snowball against the door; and the boys took to their heels. Henry was laughing as heartily[2] as he could, to think what a fool he had made of George.

George had a whipping for his folly, as he ought to have had. He was such a coward, that he was afraid of being called a coward. He did not dare refuse[3] to do as Henry told him, for fear that he would be laughed at.

If he had been really a brave boy, he would have said, "Henry, do you suppose that I am so foolish as to throw that snowball, just

---

1 Credit, *reputation.*
2 Heartily, *freely, merrily.*
3 Refuse, *decline.*

because you want to have me? You may throw your own snowballs, if you please!"

Henry would, perhaps, have laughed at him, and called him a coward.

But George would have said, "Do you think that I care for your laughing? I do not think it right to throw the snowball. I will not do that which I think to be wrong, if the whole town should join with you in laughing."

This would have been real courage. Henry would have seen, at once, that it would do no good to laugh at a boy who had so bold a heart. You must have this fearless[1] spirit, or you will get into trouble, and will be, and ought to be, disliked[2] by all.

【中文阅读】

　　一个寒冷的冬日，三个男孩经过一座校舍。年纪最大的那个是个坏男孩，不但自己惹麻烦，还试图把别人也扯进去。年纪最小的那个，名叫乔治，是个很乖的男孩子。

　　乔治愿意做正确的事情，但是非常缺乏勇气。另外两个男孩，一个叫亨利，一个叫詹姆斯。他们在路上走的时候，谈话内容是这样的：

　　亨利：要是扔一个雪球去砸教室的门，让老师和学生都吓得跳起来，那该多好玩啊！

　　詹姆斯：你这么做的话，跳起来的那个人就是你！就算老师没有抓住你，用鞭子抽你，他也会告诉你爸爸，那样你也得挨一顿打。我想，那会让你比那些学生跳得更高。

　　亨利：什么呀，老师还没开门出来，我们已经跑得老远了。他根本就分辨不清我们是谁。这儿有个像冰块一样硬的雪球。而且，乔治会很乐意把它砸到门上的。

　　詹姆斯：把雪球给他，看看怎么样。他才不敢扔呢。

　　亨利：你以为乔治是个胆小鬼吗？你没有我那么了解他。来，乔治，拿着

---

1 Fearless, *bold, brave.*

2 Disliked, *not loved.*

这个雪球，让詹姆斯看看你并不像他所想的那样是个胆小鬼。

乔治：我不是不敢扔，而是我不想这么做。我不认为这么做对我有任何好处，也看不出这有什么好玩。

詹姆斯：看吧！我告诉你他不敢扔。

亨利：不是吧，乔治，你真的变成胆小鬼了吗？我以为你什么都不怕。来吧，挽回你的荣誉，把雪球扔出去。我知道你并不是害怕。

乔治：好吧，我并不害怕。把雪球给我。我很乐意把它扔出去。

"砰"的一声，一击即中！雪球砸在门上。那两个男孩马上溜之大吉。亨利想到愚弄乔治的情景，尽情地哈哈大笑。

乔治为他的愚蠢挨了一顿打，一如他应该受到的惩罚。他真是个胆小鬼，他担心别人说他是胆小鬼，不敢拒绝亨利叫他做的事情，因为害怕会因此受到嘲笑。

如果他真是个勇敢的孩子，他应该说："亨利，你以为我会那么笨，只是因为你想要我扔那个雪球，我就会照做吗？你要是愿意的话，你完全可以自己扔！"

也许，亨利会嘲笑他，叫他胆小鬼。

然而乔治可以说："你以为我会在乎你的嘲笑吗？我认为扔这个球是不对的。我不会去做我认为是错的事情，哪怕全镇的人都跟你一起嘲笑我。"

这才是真正的勇气。亨利马上就会看到，嘲笑一个有着如此勇敢的一颗心的男孩没有任何好处。你必须有这种无畏的精神，否则你会陷入麻烦当中，而你将会、也应该会，为所有人所不耻。

LESSON 53
THE OLD CLOCK

◆

老时钟

1. In the old, old hall the old clock stands,
   And round and round move the steady hands;
   With its tick, tick, tick, both night and day,
   While seconds and minutes pass away.

2. At the old, old clock oft wonders Nell,
   For she can't make out what it has to tell;
   She has ne'er yet read, in prose[1] or rhyme[2],
   That it marks the silent course of time.

3. When I was a child, as Nell is now,
   And long ere Time had wrinkled[3] my brow[4],
   The old, old clock both by night and day
   Said,—"Tick, tick, tick!" Time passes away.

【中文阅读】

1. 在很旧的大厅里立着一座老时钟，
   沉稳的指针一圈一圈在走动，
   伴随着滴答、滴答、滴答，夜以继日，
   一秒一秒、一分一分，随之流逝。

2. 站在古老的时钟前，内尔满脸困惑，
   她无法理解它的诉说，
   她未曾读懂，散文或韵律诗，
   说时钟标记着时间沉默的轨迹。

3. 我还是个孩子时就像内尔这样，
   很久以前，时间还没把皱纹刻在我额头，
   古老的时钟同样夜以继日地说：
   "滴答，滴答，滴答！" 时间匆匆而过。

---

1 Prose, *the common language of men in talking or writing.*

2 Rhyme, *verse, poetry.*

3 Wrinkled, *having creases or folds in the skin.*

4 Brow, *the forehead.*

LESSON 54

THE WAVES

———◇———

海　浪

1. "Where are we to go?" said the little waves to the great, deep sea.

"Go, my darlings, to the yellow sands: you will find work to do there."

2. "I want to play," said one little wave; "I want to see who can jump the highest."

"No; come on, come on," said an earnest wave; "mother must be right. I want to work."

3. "Oh, I dare not go," said another; "look at those great, black rocks close to the sands; I dare not go there, for they will tear me to pieces."

4. "Take my hand, sister," said the earnest wave; "let us go on together. How glorious it is to do some work."

5. "Shall we ever go back to mother?" "Yes, when our work is done."

6. So one and all hurried on. Even the little wave that wanted to play, pressed[1] on, and thought that work might be fun after all. The timid[2] ones did not like to be left behind, and they became earnest as they got nearer the sands.

7. After all, it was fun, pressing on one after another—jumping, laughing, running on to the broad, shining sands.

8. First, they came in their course to a great sand castle. Splash, splash! they all went over it, and down it came. "Oh, what fun!" they cried.

9. "Mother told me to bring these seaweeds; I will find a pretty place for them," said one—and she ran a long way over the sands, and left them among the pebbles. The pebbles cried, "We are glad you are come. We wanted washing."

10. "Mother sent these shells; I don't know where to put them," said a

---

1 Pressed, *pushed, followed closely.*

2 Timid, *wanting courage, not bold.*

little fretful[1] wave. "Lay them one by one on the sand, and do not break them," said the eldest[2] wave.

11. And the little one went about its work, and learned to be quiet and gentle, for fear of breaking the shells.

12. "Where is my work?" said a great, full-grown wave. "This is mere play. The little ones can do this and laugh over it. Mother said there was work for me." And he came down upon some large rocks.

13. Over the rocks and into a pool he went, and he heard the fishes say, "The sea is coming. Thank you, great sea; you always send a big wave when a storm is nigh. Thank you, kind wave; we are all ready for you now."

14. Then the waves all went back over the wet sands, slowly and carelessly, for they were tired.

15. "All my shells are safe," said one.

16. And, "My seaweeds are left behind," said another.

17. "I washed all of the pebbles," said a third.

18. "And I—I only broke on a rock, and splashed into a pool," said the one

---

1 Fretful, *cross, peevish.*
2 Eldest, *first, foremost.*

that was so eager to work. "I have done no good, mother—no work at all."

19. "Hush!" said the sea. And they heard a child that was walking on the shore, say, "O mother, the sea has been here! Look, how nice and clean the sand is, and how clear the water is in that pool."

20. Then the sea, said, "Hark!" and far away they heard the deep moaning[1] of the coming storm.

21. "Come, my darlings," said she; "you have done your work, now let the storm do its work."

【中文阅读】

1. "我们要去哪里？"小海浪们对伟大而深沉的海说。

"去吧……亲爱的，去那黄色的沙滩，你们会在那里找到可以做的事情的。"

2. "我想玩耍，"其中一朵小海浪说，"我想看看谁能跳得最高。"

"不，来吧，来吧，"一朵充满干劲的海浪说，"母亲一定是对的。我想要做些事情。"

3. "噢，我不敢去，"另外一朵说，"看那些靠近沙滩的巨大的、黑黑的岩石，我不敢到那里去，因为他们会把我撕成碎片的。"

4. "拉着我的手，妹妹，"充满干劲的海浪说，"我们一起去。有所作为是多么光荣！"

5. "我们还能回到妈妈身边吗？""会的，当我们完成任务之后。"

6. 于是所有海浪都赶紧前往。甚至那朵只想玩耍的小海浪也紧随而去，心想任务也许终究是有趣的。胆小的那些不愿意被甩在后面，于是在更接近沙滩的时候，他们变得充满干劲。

7. 毕竟，那是有趣的，一个紧跟着一个——跳跃、欢笑、奔跑，向着宽阔、闪闪发光的沙滩进发。

8. 在前进的道路上，他们首先奔向一座了不起的城堡。飞溅，飞溅！他们全都越过了城堡，城堡坍塌了。"噢，多好玩！"他们喊叫着。

9. "母亲叫我把这些海藻带来，我会为他们找个好地方的。"一朵海浪说，她在沙滩上跑了很长的路，把海藻留在了卵石之间。卵石们呼喊道："我们很高

---

1 Moaning, *making a low, dull sound, muttering.*

兴你们来了。我们需要清洁。"

10. "母亲让我们送这些贝壳，我不知道该把他们放哪里。"一朵焦躁的小海浪说。"把他们一个个放在沙滩上，不要打碎他们。"最前面的海浪告诉她。

11. 小的那朵带着她的任务去了，学着安静而温柔地行动，生怕打碎了那些贝壳。

12. "我的任务在哪里？"一朵巨大的、成长完全的海浪问。"我现在这样只是玩。那些小的海浪都可以做这个事情并且一笑了之。母亲说有任务专门给'我'的。"说着他落到一些巨大的岩石上。

13. 他越过岩石，来到了一个池子里，这时他听到鱼儿说："海水来了。谢谢你，伟大的海。每当暴风雨临近的时候，你总是送来一个巨浪。谢谢，仁慈的海浪；现在我们全都准备好了，迎接你的到来。"

14. 之后，所有海浪都越过潮湿的沙滩往回走，他们走得很慢，漫不经心，因为他们都累了。

15. "我所有的贝壳都安然无恙。"一个说。

16. "还有我的海藻也留在那里了。"另一个说。

17. "我清洗了所有的卵石。"第三个说。

18. "而我——我只是撞击到一块岩石上，然后溅落到一个池子里，"那朵最急于要有所作为的浪花说，"我没有做好，母亲——我没有完成任何任务。"

19. "嘘！"大海示意。他们听见一个在岸边走着的孩子说："噢，妈妈，海水来过这里！看，沙滩多干净多好，还有那个池子里的水多么清澈！"

20. 然后，大海又说："听！"他们听到遥远的地方传来即将到来的暴风雨低沉的呻吟。

21. "来吧，我亲爱的孩子们，"她说，"你们已经完成了你们的任务，现在让暴风雨来做他的工作吧。"

LESSON 55

DON'T KILL THE BIRDS

◇

不要杀害鸟类

1. Don't kill the birds! the little birds,
   That sing about your door
   Soon as the joyous Spring has come,
   And chilling storms are o'er.

2. The little birds! how sweet they sing!
   Oh, let them joyous live;
   And do not seek to take the life
   Which you can never give.

3. Don't kill the birds! the pretty birds,
   That play among the trees;
   For earth would be a cheerless place,
   If it were not for these.

4. The little birds! how fond they play!
   Do not disturb[1] their sport;
   But let them warble[2] forth their songs,
   Till winter cuts them short.

5. Don't kill the birds! the happy birds,
   That bless the field and grove;

---

1 Disturb, *interfere with*.

2 Warble, *to trill, to carol.*

So innocent[1] to look upon,
    They claim our warmest love.

6. The happy birds, the tuneful[2] birds,
    How pleasant 't is to see!
    No spot can be a cheerless place
    Where'er their presence[3] be.

【中文阅读】

1. 不要杀害鸟类！弱小的鸟，
    它们在你门前歌唱，
    当欢乐的春天来临，
    寒冷的暴风雨已成过往。

2. 小鸟儿！它们的歌声多甜美！
    噢，让它们做快乐的生灵。
    不要试图夺走，
    你从未给予的生命。

---

1 Innocent, *pure, harmless.*
2 Tuneful, *musical, melodious.*
3 Presence, *state of being at hand, existence.*

3. 不要杀害鸟类！那美丽的鸟儿，
   它们在林间玩耍，
   如果没有了它们，
   地球上的乐趣将会多么匮乏。

4. 小鸟儿们！它们玩得多么高兴！
   请勿打扰它们的游戏；
   让它们唱出柔和的颤音，
   直到因为冬天来临中断为止。

5. 不要杀害鸟类！那快乐的小鸟，
   它们把田野和果园守护；
   你看它们如此天真无辜，
   值得我们最热忱的爱慕。

6. 开心的小鸟，音调悦耳的小鸟，
   看见它们多么令人愉悦神往！
   有它们出现的所在，
   不会是缺少喜乐的地方。

LESSON 56

WHEN TO SAY NO

———◇———

什么时候说不

1. Though "No" is a very little word, it is not always easy to say it; and the not doing so, often causes[1] trouble.

2. When we are asked to stay away from school, and spend in idleness[2] or mischief the time which ought to be spent in study, we should at once say "No."

3. When we are urged[3] to loiter[4] on our way to school, and thus be late, and interrupt[5] our teacher and the school, we should say "No." When some schoolmate wishes us to whisper or play in the schoolroom, we should say "No."

4. When we are tempted[6] to use angry or wicked words, we should remember that the eye of God is always upon us, and should say "No."

5. When we have done anything wrong, and are tempted to conceal[7] it by falsehood[8], we should say "No, we can not tell a lie; it is wicked and cowardly."

6. If we are asked to do anything which we know to be wrong, we should not fear to say "No."

7. If we thus learn to say "No," we shall avoid much trouble, and be always safe.

---

1 Causes, *makes.*

2 Idleness, *a doing nothing, laziness.*

3 Urged, *asked repeatedly.*

4 Loiter, *linger, delay.*

5 Interrupt, *disturb, hinder.*

6 Tempted, *led by evil circumstances.*

7 Conceal, *hide.*

8 Falsehood, *untruth.*

【中文阅读】

1. 虽然"不"是个非常简单的词语,可是要说出来并不总是容易的;而不把它说出来,常常会引来麻烦。

2. 如果有人叫我们逃学,懒散度日或者把应该用于学习的时间用来调皮捣蛋,我们应该马上说"不"。

3. 当有人怂恿我们在上学的路上消磨时间,从而迟到、打断老师上课或者学校的活动,我们应该说"不"。当有的同学想要我们在教室里交头接耳或玩耍,我们应该说"不"。

4. 当我们受到诱惑,想要使用愤怒或邪恶的言语时,我们应该记住上帝的眼睛无时无刻不在注视着我们,我们应该说"不"。

5. 当我们做了错事,却想要用谎话来掩饰时,我们应该说"不,我们不能说谎,那是邪恶而懦弱的行为。"

6. 要是有人要求我们做任何我们知道是错的事情,我们应该勇敢无畏地说"不"。

7. 如果我们就此学会说"不",我们将会避免许多麻烦,长享平安。

LESSON 57

WHICH LOVED BEST

◇

谁最爱

1. "I love you, mother," said little John;
   Then, forgetting work, his cap went on,
   And he was off to the garden swing,
   Leaving his mother the wood to bring.

2. "I love you, mother," said rosy Nell;
   "I love you better than tongue can tell;"
   Then she teased and pouted full half the day,
   Till her mother rejoiced when she went to play.

3. "I love you, mother," said little Fan;
   "To-day I'll help you all I can;
   How glad I am that school doesn't keep!"
   So she rocked the baby till it fell asleep.

4. Then, stepping softly, she took the broom,
   And swept the floor, and dusted the room;
   Busy and happy all day was she,
   Helpful and cheerful as child could be.

5. "I love you, mother," again they said—
   Three little children going to bed;
   How do you think that mother guessed
   Which of them really loved her best?

(Joy Allison)

【中文阅读】

1. "我爱你，妈妈，"小约翰说，
   他戴上帽子，忘掉了干活，
   他来到花园里荡秋千，
   留下他的妈妈拣拾木片。

2. "我爱你，妈妈，"罗斯·内尔说，
   "我比语言能表达的爱你更多。"
   整整半天她不是捉弄人就是发脾气，
   直到她出去玩妈妈才高兴地松一口气。

3. "我爱你，妈妈，"小范说，
   "今天我会尽我所能帮你干活，
   我多高兴今天不用上学校！"
   然后她摇晃小宝宝直到它睡着。

4. 脚步轻柔地，她去把扫帚拿起来，
　　扫干净地板，再拭去房间里的尘埃，
　　她高兴地忙活了一整日，
　　作为孩子最有用最快乐莫过如此。

5. "我爱你，妈妈，"三个小孩再次开口，
　　在他们上床睡觉的时候；
　　你猜妈妈会认为谁，
　　是他们当中最爱她的那一位？

（乔伊·艾利森）

LESSON 58

JOHN CARPENTER

◇

约翰·卡朋特

1. John Carpenter did not like to buy toys that somebody else had made. He liked the fun of making them himself. The thought that they were his own work delighted him.

2. Tom Austin, one of his playmates, thought a toy was worth nothing unless it cost a great deal of money. He never tried to make anything, but bought all his toys.

3. "Come and look at my horse," said he, one day. "It cost a dollar, and it is such a beauty! Come and see it."

4. John was soon admiring[1] his friend's horse; and he was examining[2] it carefully, to see how it was made. The same evening he began to make one for himself.

5. He went into the wood shed, and picked out two pieces of wood—one for the head of his horse, the other for the body. It took him two or three days to shape them to his satisfaction.

6. His father gave him a bit of red leather[3] for a bridle, and a few brass nails, and his mother found a bit of old fur with which he made a mane and tail for his horse.

7. But what about the wheels? This puzzled[4] him. At last he thought he would go to a turner's[5] shop, and see if he could not get some round pieces of wood which might suit his purpose.

8. He found a large number of such pieces among the shavings[6] on the floor, and asked permission[7] to take a few of them. The turner asked him what he wanted them for, and he told him about his horse.

9. "Oh," said the man, laughing, "if you wish it, I will make some wheels for your horse. But mind, when it is finished, you must let me see it."

10. John promised to do so, and he soon ran home with the wheels in his pocket. The next evening, he went to the turner's shop with his horse all complete[8], and was told that he was an ingenious[9] little fellow.

11. Proud of this compliment[10], he ran to his friend Tom, crying, "Now then, Tom, here is my horse,—look!"

12. "Well, that is a funny horse," said Tom; "where did you buy it?" "I didn't buy it," replied John; "I made it."

13. "You made it yourself! Oh, well, it's a good horse for you to make. But it is not so good as mine. Mine cost a dollar, and yours didn't cost anything."

---

1 Admiring, *looking at with pleasure.*
2 Examining, *looking at every point.*
3 Leather, *the skin of an animal prepared for use.*
4 Puzzled, *perplexed, caused trouble.*
5 Turner's, *one who shapes wooden or metal articles by means of a lathe.*
6 Shavings, *the thin ribbon of wood which a carpenter makes in planing.*
7 Permission, *privilege, consent.*
8 Complete, *finished.*
9 Ingenious, *skillful.*
10 Compliment, *praise, approbation.*

14. "It was real fun to make it, though," said John, and away he ran with his horse rolling after him.

15. Do you want to know what became of John? Well, I will tell you. He studied hard in school, and was called the best scholar in his class. When he left school, he went to work in a machine shop. He is now a master workman, and will soon have a shop of his own.

【中文阅读】

1. 约翰·卡朋特不喜欢买那些别人做的玩具。他喜欢享受自己动手制作玩具的乐趣。想到那是自己的作品，他就会高兴。

2. 汤姆·奥斯汀是他的一个玩伴，他认为一件玩具除非是花很多钱买回来的，否则就一文不值。他从来不会自己做任何东西，所有的玩具都是买回来的。

3. "来看我的马，"有一天，他说，"它值一美元呢，它是多么漂亮啊！快来看！"

4. 很快约翰就喜欢上了朋友的马，他认真地查看，观察它是怎么做成的。当天晚上，他就开始自己动手做一个。

5. 他走进木棚，挑了两块木头——一块用来做马头，另一块做马的身子。他花了两三天才做出自己满意的造型。

6. 他的父亲给了他一点红色的皮革做缰绳，还给了他一些铜钉，母亲帮他找到一小片旧的毛皮，他用这个做了马的鬃毛和尾巴。

7. 可是车轮怎么办呢？这可把他难住了。最后他想可以到车工的店里，看看是否能找到圆形的木片，也许可以达到他的目的。

8. 他在地上的刨花堆里找到了很多这样的木片，征得同意后他拿了一些。车工问他要这些木片来做什么，他跟他说起了他的马。

9. "噢，"那个人笑着说，"你要是想要，我可以为你的小马做几个轮子。不过要记住，你做好以后，要给我看看。"

10. 约翰答应了，很快他就带着装在口袋里的轮子跑回家去了。第二天晚上，他带着完成了的马去车工的店里，车工夸他是个心灵手巧的小家伙。

11. 这样的夸奖让约翰很自豪，他跑到好朋友汤姆那里，大声说："现在看看，汤姆，这是我的马——看！"

12. "嗯，这匹马很有趣，"汤姆说，"你在哪里买的？""我没有花钱买，"汤姆回答，"我做的。"

13. "你自己做的！噢，好吧，你做的马不错。不过没有我的好。我的马值一美元，你的一分钱都不值。"

14. "但是自己制作真的很有意思。"说完约翰就跑开了，他的马在身后跟着他滚动。

15. 你想知道约翰后来成为什么样的人吗？好，我来告诉你。他在学校里努力学习，被称为他们班上最好的学生。离开学校后，他去了一个机械修理店工作。现在他已经是一个工长，而且很快就要拥有他自己的店了。

LESSON 59

PERSEVERE

◇

持之以恒

1. The fisher who draws in his net too soon,
   Won't have any fish to sell;
   The child who shuts up his book too soon,
   Won't learn any lessons well.

2. If you would have your learning stay,
   Be patient,—don't learn too fast:
   The man who travels a mile each day,
   May get round the world at last.

【中文阅读】

1. 渔夫太快收网，
   什么鱼也没捕到；
   小孩过早合上书，
   哪课都学不好。

2. 如果你想记住学到的知识，
   耐心——不要学得太匆忙；
   一个人每天走一英里，
   总有一天会走遍世界。

LESSON 60

THE CONTENTED BOY

◆

知足的男孩

Mr. Lenox was one morning riding by himself. He got off from his horse to look at something on the roadside. The horse broke away from him, and ran off. Mr. Lenox ran after him, but soon found that he could not catch him.

A little boy at work in a field near the road, heard the horse. As soon as he saw him running from his master, the boy ran very quickly to the middle of the road, and, catching the horse by the bridle, stopped him till Mr. Lenox came up.

Mr. Lenox. Thank you, my good boy, you have caught my horse very nicely. What shall I give you for your trouble?

Boy. I want nothing, sir.

Mr. L. You want nothing? So much the better for you. Few men can say as much. But what were you doing in the field?

B. I was rooting[1] up weeds, and tending[2] the sheep that were feeding on turnips[3].

Mr. L. Do you like to work?

B. Yes, sir, very well, this fine weather[4].

Mr. L. But would you not rather play?

B. This is not hard work. It is almost as good as play.

Mr. L. Who set you to work?

B. My father, sir.

Mr. L. What is your name?

B. Peter Hurdle, sir.

---

1 Rooting, *pulling up by the roots.*

2 Tending, *watching, attending.*

3 Turnips, *a vegetable.*

4 Weather, *state of the atmosphere.*

Mr. L. How old are you?

B. Eight years old, next June.

Mr. L. How long have you been here?

B. Ever since six o'clock this morning.

Mr. L. Are you not hungry?

B. Yes, sir, but I shall go to dinner soon.

Mr. L. If you had a dime now, what would you do with it?

B. I don't know, sir. I never had so much.

Mr. L. Have you no playthings?

B. Playthings? What are they?

Mr. L. Such things as ninepins, marbles, tops, and wooden horses.

B. No, sir. Tom and I play at football in winter, and I have a jumping rope. I had a hoop, but it is broken.

Mr. L. Do you want nothing else?

B. I have hardly time to play with what I have. I have to drive the cows, and to run on errands[1], and to ride the horses to the fields, and that is as good as play.

Mr. L. You could get apples and cakes, if you had money, you know.

---

1 Errands, *messages.*

B. I can have apples at home. As for cake, I do not want that. My mother makes me a pie now and then, which is as good.

Mr. L. Would you not like a knife to cut sticks?

B. I have one. Here it is. Brother Tom gave it to me.

Mr. L. Your shoes are full of holes. Don't you want a new pair?

B. I have a better pair for Sundays.

Mr. L. But these let in water.

B. I do not mind that, sir.

Mr. L. Your hat is all torn, too.

B. I have a better one at home.

Mr. L. What do you do when it rains?

B. If it rains very hard when I am in the field, I get under a tree for shelter.

Mr. L. What do you do, if you are hungry before it is time to go home?

B. I sometimes eat a raw[1] turnip.

Mr. L. But if there is none?

B. Then I do as well as I can without. I work on, and never think of it.

Mr. L. Why, my little fellow, I am glad to see that you are so contented. Were you ever at school?

B. No, sir. But father means to send me next winter.

Mr. L. You will want books then.

B. Yes, sir; each boy has a Spelling Book, a Reader, and a Testament[2].

Mr. L. Then I will give them to you. Tell your father so, and that it is because you are an obliging, contented little boy.

B. I will, sir. Thank you.

Mr. L. Good by, Peter.

B. Good morning, sir.

(Dr. John Aiken)

【中文阅读】

　　有一天早晨，雷诺克斯先生正独自骑着马。为了看路旁的某样东西，他从

---

1 Raw, *not cooked.*

2 Testament, *the last twenty-seven books of the Bible.*

马上下来了。突然，马从他手上挣脱，跑开了。雷诺克斯先生急忙去追，可是很快就发现不可能追得上。

　　路旁的田里有一个小男孩正在劳作，他听到了马的声音。他一看到马从主人身边逃开，就迅速跑到路中间，他抓住了缰绳，让马停了下来，等待雷克诺斯先生走近。

　　雷诺克斯先生（以下为"雷"）：谢谢你，好小伙儿，你抓住了我的马，干得很漂亮。给你添了麻烦，我该给你些什么表示感谢呢？

　　男孩（以下为"男"）：我什么也不要，先生。

　　雷：你什么也不要？对你来说何乐而不为呢。很少有人能这么说的。可是你刚才在田里做什么呢？

　　男：我在除草，还有照看吃芜菁的绵羊。

　　雷：你喜欢干活吗？

　　男：是的，先生，很喜欢，这么好的天气。

　　雷：可是你不想去玩耍吗？

　　男：这不是什么重活，这几乎和玩耍一样好。

　　雷：是谁安排你来干活的？

　　男：我的父亲，先生。

　　雷：你叫什么名字？

　　男：彼得·赫德尔，先生。

　　雷：你多大了？

　　男：到6月就8岁了。

　　雷：你在这儿待了多久了？

　　男：早晨6点以后我就一直在这里。

　　雷：你肚子不饿吗？

　　男：饿的，先生，但是我很快就要吃午饭了。

　　雷：如果你有个一角的硬币，你会用它来做什么呢？

　　男：我不知道，先生，我从来没有过那么多的钱。

　　雷：你没有玩具吗？

　　男：玩具？玩具是什么？

　　雷：例如九柱戏、玻璃弹子、陀螺和木马等。

　　男：没有，先生。汤姆和我冬天的时候玩橄榄球，我有一根跳绳，还有一个铁箍，不过坏掉了。

雷：你不想要点别的东西吗？

男：我几乎没有时间玩我拥有的东西。我必须赶牛、跑腿、把马骑到田野里放养，这些事情和玩一样有趣。

雷：你知道，如果你有钱，可以买到苹果和蛋糕。

男：我家里就有苹果。至于说蛋糕，我不想要。我妈妈时不时会为我做馅饼，那也一样好吃。

雷：你想不想要一把刀用来削木棍？

男：我有一把。就在这儿。汤姆哥哥给我的。

雷：你的鞋子全是洞，难道你不想要一双新的吗？

男：我有一双好一点的鞋子，星期天才穿的。

雷：可是你现在穿的这双会进水的。

男：我不介意，先生。

雷：你的帽子也破了。

男：我家里有一顶更好的。

雷：下雨的时候你怎么办呢？

男：我在地里干活的时候，要是雨下得很大，我就到树底下避一避。

雷：如果你饿了，可是还没到时间回家，你怎么办？

男：我有时候会吃一个生萝卜。

雷：要是没有生萝卜呢？

男：那没有东西吃我也会一样好好地干活。我会继续干活，不去想它。

雷：啊，我的小家伙，我很高兴看到你如此知足常乐。你有没有上过学？

男：没有，先生。不过父亲有意明年冬天送我去念书。

雷：到那时你会需要书本的。

男：是的，先生。每个男孩都会有拼写课本、阅读课本和《圣经》。

雷：那么到时我会给你这些东西。把我的话转告你的父亲，并且告诉他，这是因为你是个乐于助人、知足常乐的小男孩。

男：我会的，先生。谢谢！

雷：再见，彼得。

男：愿您有个愉快的早上，先生。

（约翰·艾肯博士）

LESSON 61
LITTLE GUSTAVA

◇

小古斯塔瓦

1. Little Gustava[1] sits in the sun,
   Safe in the porch, and the little drops run
   From the icicles[2] under the eaves[3] so fast,
   For the bright spring sun shines warm at last,
        And glad is little Gustava.

2. She wears a quaint[4] little scarlet cap,
   And a little green bowl she holds in her lap,
   Filled with bread and milk to the brim,
   And a wreath of marigolds[5] round the rim:
        "Ha! ha!" laughs little Gustava.

3. Up comes her little gray, coaxing cat,
   With her little pink nose, and she mews, "What's that?"
   Gustava feeds her,—she begs for more,
   And a little brown hen walks in at the door:
        "Good day!" cries little Gustava.

4. She scatters crumbs for the little brown hen,
   There comes a rush and a flutter, and then

---

1 Gustava, *a girl's name.*

2 Icicles, *water frozen in long needle-like shapes.*

3 Eaves, *the lower edges of a roof.*

4 Quaint, *odd.*

5 Marigolds, *a yellow flower.*

Down fly her little white doves so sweet,
With their snowy wings and their crimson feet:
        "Welcome!" cries little Gustava.

5. So dainty and eager they pick up the crumbs.
   But who is this through the doorway comes?
   Little Scotch terrier, little dog Rags,
   Looks in her face, and his funny tail wags:
        "Ha! ha!" laughs little Gustava.

6. "You want some breakfast, too?" and down
   She sets her bowl on the brick floor brown,
   And little dog Rags drinks up her milk,
   While she strokes his shaggy locks, like silk:
        "Dear Rags!" says little Gustava.

7. Waiting without stood sparrow and crow,
   Cooling their feet in the melting snow.
   "Won't you come in, good folk?" she cried,
   But they were too bashful, and staid outside,
       Though "Pray come in!" cried Gustava.

8. So the last she threw them, and knelt[1] on the mat,
   With doves, and biddy[2], and dog, and cat.
   And her mother came to the open house door:
   "Dear little daughter, I bring you some more,
       My merry little Gustava."

9. Kitty and terrier, biddy and doves,
   All things harmless Gustava loves,
   The shy, kind creatures 't is joy to feed,
   And, oh! her breakfast is sweet indeed
       To happy little Gustava!

                                            (*Celia Thaxter*)

【中文阅读】

1. 小古斯塔瓦安然坐在阳光下，
   她在门廊里，屋檐上冰柱悬挂，
   水珠点点滴滴飞快落下来，
   明亮的春日暖阳终于照耀户外，
   小古斯塔瓦笑逐颜开。

2. 她头戴别致的小红帽，
   膝盖上托着一个绿碗很小巧，
   面包和牛奶满到碗的边缘，

---

1 Knelt, *bent on her knees.*
2 Biddy, *chicken.*

边上是一圈金盏花的图案，

"哈！哈！"小古斯塔瓦笑得欢。

3. 她那会哄人的小灰猫来了，

抽动粉红色的鼻子，喵喵问道："那是什么？"

古斯塔瓦喂它吃了一些，它想要更多，

一只棕色的小母鸡走进来在门前轻踱，

"日安！"小古斯塔瓦大声说。

4. 她把面包渣儿撒向小母鸡，

它拍打翅膀飞奔而至，

接着引得可爱的小白鸽俯冲而来，

它们有深红色的脚，羽毛雪白，

"欢迎！"小古斯塔瓦欢呼起来。

5. 它们急匆匆美滋滋地啄食碎面包，

可那又是谁来了，正穿过门道？

苏格兰短脚卷毛狗走了过来，

他有趣的尾巴摇摇摆摆，

"哈！哈！"小古斯塔瓦笑得好开怀。

6. "你也想吃点早餐吗？"

她把碗在褐色的砖地上放下，

小狗"抹布"喝光了她的牛奶，

她抓他蓬松的毛毛，像柔软的绸带，

"亲爱的抹布！"小古斯塔瓦语调轻快。

7. 没人等待站着的麻雀和乌鸦，

它们在融化的雪里凉着脚丫。

"你们不进来吗，善良的居民？"她呼唤，

可是它们太害羞，宁愿留在外面，

"请进来吧！"古斯塔瓦还是大声喊。

8. 最后她把所有食物都往外抛，
   跪在垫子上陪着鸽子、小鸡、小狗和小猫，
   打开屋门出来了她的妈妈，
   "亲爱的小女儿，我再给你添一些吧，
   我快乐的小古斯塔瓦。"

9. 母鸡和鸽子，小狗和猫崽，
   一切无害的动物古斯塔瓦都喜爱，
   喂养害羞、善良的生物真是赏心乐事，
   还有，噢，她的旦餐确实太好吃，
   向快乐的小古斯塔瓦致意！

（西莉亚·萨克斯特）

LESSON 62

THE INSOLENT BOY

◆

无礼的男孩

1. James Selton was one of the most insolent[1] boys in the village where he lived. He would rarely[2] pass people in the street without being guilty of some sort of abuse[3].

2. If a person were well dressed he would cry out, "Dandy[4]!" If a person's clothes were dirty or torn, he would throw stones at him, and annoy him in every way.

3. One afternoon, just as the school was dismissed[5], a stranger passed through the village. His dress was plain and somewhat old, but neat and clean. He carried a cane in his hand, on the end of which was a bundle, and he wore a broad-brimmed hat.

4. No sooner did James see the stranger, than he winked to his playmates, and said, "Now for some fun!" He then silently went toward the stranger from behind, and, knocking off his hat, ran away.

5. The man turned and saw him, but James was out of hearing before he could speak. The stranger put on his hat, and went on his way. Again did James approach; but this time, the man caught him by the arm, and held him fast.

6. However, he contented himself with looking James a moment in the face, and then pushed him from him. No sooner did the naughty[6] boy find himself free again, than he began to pelt the stranger with dirt

---

1 Insolent, *rude, insulting.*

2 Rarely, *hardly ever.*

3 Abuse, *ill usage.*

4 Dandy, *a fop.*

5 Dismissed, *let out.*

6 Naughty, *bad, wicked.*

and stones.

7. But he was much frightened when the "rowdy[1]," as he foolishly called the man, was struck on the head by a brick, and badly hurt. All the boys now ran away, and James skulked[2] across the fields to his home.

8. As he drew near the house, his sister Caroline came out to meet him, holding up a beautiful gold chain and some new books for him to see.

9. She told James, as fast as she could talk, that their uncle[3], who had been away several years, had come home, and was now in the house; that he had brought beautiful presents for the whole family; that he had left his carriage at the tavern[4], a mile or two off, and walked on foot, so as to

---

1 Rowdy, *a low fellow, who engages in fights.*
2 Skulked, *went in a sneaking manner.*
3 Uncle, *the brother of one's father or mother.*
4 Tavern, *a small hotel.*

surprise his brother, their father.

10. She said, that while he was coming through the village, some wicked boys threw stones at him, and hit him just over the eye, and that mother had bound up the wound. "But what makes you look so pale?" asked Caroline, changing her tone.

11. The guilty boy told her that nothing was the matter with him; and running into the house, he went upstairs into his chamber. Soon after, he heard his father calling him to come down. Trembling from head to foot, he obeyed. When he reached the parlor door, he stood, fearing to enter.

12. His mother said, "James, why do you not come in? You are not usually so bashful. See this beautiful watch, which your uncle has brought for you."

13. What a sense of shame did James now feel! Little Caroline seized his arm, and pulled him into the room. But he hung down his head, and covered his face with his hands.

14. His uncle went up to him, and kindly taking away his hands, said, "James, will you not bid me welcome?" But quickly starting back, he cried, "Brother, this is not your son. It is the boy who so shamefully[1] insulted[2] me in the street!"

15. With surprise and grief did the good father and mother learn this. His uncle was ready to forgive him, and forget the injury[3]. But his father would never permit James to have the gold watch, nor the beautiful books, which his uncle had brought for him.

16. The rest of the children were loaded with presents. James was obliged to content himself with seeing them happy. He never forgot this lesson so long as he lived. It cured him entirely[4] of his low and insolent manners.

【中文阅读】

1. 詹姆斯·塞尔顿是他们村子里最无礼的男孩之一。他在街上和人们迎

---

1 Shamefully, *disgracefully.*

2 Insulted, *treated with abuse.*

3 Injury, *harm done.*

4 Entirely, *altogether.*

面而过的时候，很少不犯出言不逊的过错。

2. 如果有人穿得很讲究，他会大声地叫："花花公子！"要是有人的衣服弄脏了或是被撕破了，他会向他扔石头，想尽办法激怒他。

3. 一天下午，刚刚放学的时候，有一个陌生人经过村庄。他衣着普通，显得有点旧，但干净整齐。手里拿着一根拐杖，拐杖的末端有个包袱，头上戴着一顶宽边帽。

4. 詹姆斯一看见这个陌生人，就向他的玩伴使了个眼色，说："这下有好戏看了！"然后他默不作声地从后面向那位陌生人走去，把他的帽子打下来，接着就逃跑了。

5. 那个人转过身来看着他，可是在他还没来得及说话之前，詹姆斯已经跑出去好远，听不到了。陌生人把帽子戴上，继续往前走。詹姆斯又走过来了，不过这一次，陌生人抓住詹姆斯的手臂，紧紧地按住他。

6. 然而，他只是盯着詹姆斯的脸看了一会儿，就把他往前一推，松开了他。顽皮的男孩一看到自己被放了，马上就开始向陌生人投掷泥块和石头。

7. 可是当这个他口里称之为"流氓"的人被一块砖砸到头部，而且伤得很严重的时候，詹姆斯吓坏了。这时所有其他男孩都跑了，詹姆斯偷偷摸摸地越过田野，往家里走去。

8. 当他靠近屋子的时候，妹妹卡洛琳跑出来迎接他，拿着一条漂亮的金项链和几本崭新的书给他看。

9. 她用她最快的语速，告诉詹姆斯，他们几年前离开家的叔叔回来了，现在就在家里；他为全家人带了漂亮的礼物；他把马车留在了一两英里外的旅店里，走着来的，为的是要给他的哥哥、他们的爸爸一个惊喜。

10. 她说，在叔叔穿过村庄到家里来的时候，有些顽皮的小男孩向他扔石头，把他眼睛上方打伤了，妈妈帮他包扎了伤口。"可是你的脸色怎么这么苍白？"卡洛琳问，声调也变了。

11. 负罪的男孩跟她说自己没事，然后跑进屋子，上楼进了自己的房间。过了一会儿，他听到父亲喊他下楼。他浑身颤抖着，答应了。靠近客厅门口的时候，他站住了，不敢进去。

12. 他的妈妈说："詹姆斯，为什么不进来？你平常可不是这么害羞的。看见这块漂亮的手表了吗？这是你们的叔叔带回来给你的。"

13. 此时詹姆斯感到多么内疚啊！小卡洛琳抓住他的手臂，把他拉进了房间里。但是他低着头，用手捂住脸。

14. 他的叔叔走过来，温和地把他的手拿开，说："詹姆斯，你不欢迎我吗？"然而很快他就后退了，喊了起来："兄弟，这不是你的儿子。这是那个在街上无耻地侮辱我的小男孩！"

15. 爸爸妈妈知道这件事后，又惊讶又伤心。他的叔叔愿意原谅他，不追究所受的伤。但是他的父亲不允许詹姆斯拥有那只金表和那些漂亮的书，那些都是他的叔叔带回来给他的。

16. 其他孩子们都得到了丰富的礼物。詹姆斯只好心甘情愿地看着他们高兴。他在有生之年都忘不了这个教训。这件事完全纠正了他粗俗无礼的行为举止。

LESSON 63
WE ARE SEVEN

我们是七个

1. I met a little cottage girl:
   She was eight years old, she said;
   Her hair was thick with many a curl,
   That clustered[1] round her head.

2. She had a rustic[2], woodland air,
   And she was wildly clad:
   Her eyes were fair, and very fair;—
   Her beauty made me glad.

3. "Sisters and brothers, little maid,
   How many may you be?"
   "How many? Seven in all," she said,
   And, wondering, looked at me.

4. "And where are they? I pray you tell."
   She answered, "Seven are we;
   And two of us at Conway dwell,
   And two are gone to sea.

5. "Two of us in the churchyard lie,
   My sister and my brother;

---

1 Clustered, *hung in bunches.*
2 Rustic, *country-like.*

And, in the churchyard cottage, I
Dwell near them with my mother,"

6. "You say that two at Conway dwell,
   And two are gone to sea,
   Yet ye are seven! I pray you tell,
   Sweet maid, how this may be."

7. Then did the little maid reply,
   "Seven boys and girls are we;
   Two of us in the churchyard lie,
   Beneath the churchyard tree."

8. "You run about, my little maid,
   Your limbs, they are alive;
   If two are in the churchyard laid,
   Then ye are only five."

9. "Their graves are green, they may be seen,"
   The little maid replied,
   "Twelve steps or more from mother's door,
   And they are side by side.

10. "My stockings there I often knit,
    My kerchief[1] there I hem;
    And there upon the ground I sit,
    And sing a song to them.

11. "And often after sunset, sir,
    When it is light and fair,
    I take my little porringer[2],
    And eat my supper there.

12. "The first that died was sister Jane;
    In bed she moaning lay,
    Till God released[3] her from her pain;
    And then she went away.

13. "So in the churchyard she was laid;
    And, when the grass was dry,
    Together round her grave we played,
    My brother John and I.

14. "And when the ground was white with snow,
    And I could run and slide,
    My brother John was forced to go,
    And he lies by her side."

15. "How many are you, then?" said I,

---

1 Kerchief, *handkerchief.*

2 Porringer, *a small dish for soup or porridge.*

3 Released, *freed, relieved.*

"If they two are in heaven?"
Quick was the little maid's reply,
"O master! we are seven."

16. "But they are dead; those two are dead!
Their spirits are in heaven!"
'T was throwing words away: for still
The little maid would have her will,
And said, "Nay, we are seven."

(William Wordsworth)

【中文阅读】

1. 我遇到一个乡村小姑娘，
她说，她今年八岁；
卷发盘绕在她头上，
又浓又密的一堆。

2. 她散发着一种乡野气息，
衣着也土里土气；
她的眼睛很美，非常美丽，
她的美令我欣喜。

3. "你的姐妹和兄弟，小姑娘，
一共有几个？"
"有几个？一共是七个，"她讲，
望着我，满脸好奇的神色，

4. "他们在哪里？我恳求你讲一讲。"
她回答说，"我们有七个，"

"两个住在一个叫康威的地方，
两个出海当水手去了。"

5."还有两个在教堂墓地长眠，
那是我的姐姐和哥哥；
妈妈和我也住在教堂旁边，
我们的小屋靠近他们两个。"

6."你说你们有两个住在康威那里，
两个当水手去了海上，
可你们一共是七个！我恳求你，
告诉我这是怎么回事，好姑娘。"

7. 小姑娘接着回答，
"我们是七个姐妹和兄弟；
两个躺在那棵树下，
就在教堂的墓地里。"

8."你跑来又跑去，我的小姑娘，
你有灵活的手和腿；
既然有两个躺在墓地
那你们只有五个才对。"

9."看得见他们青青的坟墓，
小姑娘说道，
离屋门口只有大概十二步，
他们在一起，紧紧依靠。"

10."我经常在那里编织毛袜，
为我的手帕缝上褶边；
我常常在坟旁的地上坐下，

为他们唱首歌消遣消遣。"

11. "先生，常常在日落之后的傍晚，
　　当天还没黑，光线还亮，
　　我会带上我的小汤碗，
　　在那里把我的晚饭吃光。"

12. "简，我的姐姐最早进的坟墓，
　　她躺在床上呻吟不止，
　　直到上帝免除了她的痛苦，
　　她便从此远离。"

13. "于是她在教堂的墓地躺下，
　　当墓上的草一干，
　　我们就围着她的坟墓玩耍。
　　就是我和我的哥哥约翰。"

14. "等到大地被白雪覆盖，
　　我可以乱跑乱滑，
　　我的哥哥约翰被迫离开，
　　他就在简的身边躺下。"

15. "那你们还剩下几个？
　　既然他们两个去了天国？"我问，
　　小姑娘的回答快得很，
　　"噢，先生，我们是七个没错。"

16. "可是他们死了，那两个已经死了啊！
　　他们的灵魂在天国里！"
　　我说这些话也是白搭
　　"不，我们是七个，"小姑娘还是坚持。

（威廉·华兹华斯）

LESSON 64

MARY'S DIME

◇

玛丽的硬币

1. There! I have drawn the chairs into the right corners, and dusted the room nicely. How cold papa and mamma will be when they return from their long ride! It is not time to toast[1] the bread yet, and I am tired of reading.

2. What shall I do? Somehow, I can't help thinking about the pale face of that little beggar girl all the time. I can see the glad light filling her eyes, just as plain as I did when I laid the dime in her little dirty hand.

---

1 Toast, *to scorch until brown by the heat of a fire.*

3. How much I had thought of that dime, too! Grandpa gave it to me a whole month ago, and I had kept it ever since in my red box upstairs; but those sugar apples looked so beautiful, and were so cheap[1]—only a dime apiece[2]—that I made up my mind to have one.

4. I can see her—the beggar girl, I mean—as she stood there in front of the store, in her old hood[3] and faded[4] dress, looking at the candies laid all in a row. I wonder what made me say, "Little girl, what do you want?"

5. How she stared[5] at me, just as if nobody had spoken kindly to her before. I guess she thought I was sorry for her, for she said, so earnestly and sorrowfully[6], "I was thinking how good one of those gingerbread[7] rolls would taste. I haven't had anything to eat to-day."

6. Now, I thought to myself, "Mary Williams, you have had a good breakfast and a good dinner this day, and this poor girl has not had a mouthful. You can give her your dime; she needs it a great deal more than you do."

7. I could not resist that little girl's sorrowful, hungry look—so I dropped the dime right into her hand, and, without waiting for her to speak, walked straight away. I'm so glad I gave her the dime, if I did have to go without the apple lying there in the window, and looking just like a real one.

【中文阅读】

1. 你瞧！我把椅子都拉到合适的角落里，把房间打扫得一尘不染。爸爸妈妈长途旅行，到家的时候该是多冷啊！现在还不是时候烤面包，而我看书也已经看烦了。

2. 我该做些什么呢？不知道为什么，我总是忍不住想起那个乞讨的小女孩。我面前浮现她眼里闪耀快乐的光彩，就像当我把一角硬币放到她脏分分的

---

1 Cheap, *low in price.*

2 Apiece, *each.*

3 Hood, *a soft covering for the head.*

4 Faded, *having lost freshness of color.*

5 Stared, *looked earnestly.*

6 Sorrowfully, *full of sadness.*

7 Gingerbread, *a kind of sweet cake flavored with ginger.*

小手里时一样。

3. 我也多么惦念那个一角硬币啊！那是祖母一个月前给我的，从那以后我一直把它放在楼上的红盒子里。可是那些释迦果看起来多漂亮啊，而且那么便宜——只要一角钱一个——于是我下定决心要去买一个。

4. 我能看到她——那个乞讨的女孩，我的意思是——当时她站在商店前面，戴着旧头巾，穿着褪了色的裙子，看着那些摆成一行的糖果时，我不知道是什么促使我说："小姑娘，你想要什么？"

5. 她盯着我的神情显得多惊讶啊！就好像从来没有人和气地跟她说过话一样。我猜她是认为我为她感到难过，因为她语气急切而悲伤地答道："我在想那些姜饼卷该会有多好吃。今天我还没吃过东西。"

6. 那个时候，我在心里对自己说："玛丽·威廉斯，你今天吃了丰盛的早餐和午餐，这个可怜的小女孩却一口饭都吃不上。你可以把你那个硬币给她，她比你更需要。"

7. 我无法抗拒那个小女孩悲伤、饥饿的神情——于是我把硬币塞到她的手里，不等她开口说话，就立刻走开了。我很高兴自己把硬币给了她，就像是我确实必须走开，让那个释迦果留在橱窗里，只是看起来像真的。

LESSON 65
MARY DOW

◇

玛丽·道

1. "Come in, little stranger," I said,
   As she tapped at my half-open door;
   While the blanket[1], pinned over her head,
   Just reached to the basket she bore.

2. A look full of innocence fell
   From her modest and pretty blue eye,
   As she said, "I have matches[2] to sell,
   And hope you are willing to buy.

---

1 Blanket, *a square of loosely woven woolen cloth.*
2 Matches,*small splints of wood, one end of which has been dipped in a preparation which will take fire by rubbing.*

3. "A penny[1] a bunch is the price,
    I think you'll not find it too much;
  They are tied up so even and nice,
    And ready to light with a touch."

4. I asked, "What's your name, little girl?"
    "'Tis Mary," said she, "Mary Dow;"
  And carelessly tossed off a curl,
    That played on her delicate[2] brow.

5. "My father was lost on the deep;
    The ship never got to the shore;
  And mother is sad, and will weep,
    To hear the wind blow and sea roar.

6. "She sits there at home, without food,
    Beside our poor, sick Willy's bed;
  She paid all her money for wood,
    And so I sell matches for bread.

7. "I'd go to the yard and get chips,
    But then it would make me too sad
  To see the men building the ships,
    And think they had made one so bad.

8. "But God, I am sure, who can take
    Such fatherly care of a bird,
  Will never forget nor forsake[3]
    The children who trust in his word.

9. "And now, if I only can sell

---

1 Penny, *cent.*
2 Delicate, *soft and fair.*
3 Forsake, *leave, reject.*

The matches I brought out to-day,
I think I shall do very well,
And we shall rejoice at the pay."

10. "Fly home, little bird," then I thought,
"Fly home, full of joy, to your nest;"
For I took all the matches she brought,
And Mary may tell you the rest.

【中文阅读】

1. 当她轻轻叩响我那半开的门扇，
   "请进，小陌生人，"我开口，
   别在她头上的布毯，
   垂落到她手中的篮子里。

2. 她的蓝色眼睛美丽而害羞，
   投向我的眼神天真可爱，
   她说："我有一些火柴出售，
   希望您愿意购买。"

3. "一把火柴只要一便士，
   我想这个价钱您不会觉得很高；
   火柴捆得整整齐齐，
   轻轻一擦就能点着。"

4. 我问她："你叫什么名字，小姑娘？"
   "我叫玛丽。"她说，"姓陶，名叫玛丽。"
   一缕卷发随意滑落脸上，
   在她精致的额前嬉戏。

5. "我父亲的船没能回到岸边，
   他消失在海的深处；
   只要一听见海风海浪的声音，
   伤心的母亲就会哭。"

6. "她守在可怜的威利病床边，
   整天在家里吃不下饭；
   她买木柴就花了所有的钱，
   所以为了面包我才出来卖火柴。"

7. "我愿意到院场上捡拾碎木片，
   可是那会让我非常伤心，
   因为我会见到工人在造船，
   想起曾经有过一艘坏船夺走了父亲，"

8. "可是上帝，我深信不疑，
   能给予小鸟慈父般呵护的上帝，
   永远不会忘记，也不会放弃，
   信赖他每一句话的孩子。"

9. "现在，只要我能卖掉，
   今天带出来的这些火柴，
   我想我会做得很好，
   挣的钱会让我们感到愉快。"

10. "飞回家吧，小鸟儿，"后来我在心里独白，
    "飞回家，满怀欢乐，飞回你的巢里。"
    因为我买下了她所有的火柴，
    剩下的事情也许玛丽会告诉你。

LESSON 66
THE LITTLE LOAF

◇

小块面包

1. Once when there was a famine[1], a rich baker sent for twenty of the poorest children in the town, and said to them, "In this basket there is a loaf[2] for each of you. Take it, and come back to me every day at this hour till God sends us better times."

2. The hungry children gathered eagerly about the basket, and quarreled for the bread, because each wished to have the largest loaf. At last they

---

1 Famine, *a general scarcity of food.*

2 Loaf, *a molded mass of regular shape (as of bread or cake).*

went away without even thanking the good gentleman.

3. But Gretchen[1], a poorly-dressed little girl, did not quarrel or struggle with the rest, but remained[2] standing modestly in the distance[3]. When the ill-behaved[4] girls had left, she took the smallest loaf, which alone was left in the basket, kissed the gentleman's hand, and went home.

4. The next day the children were as ill-behaved as before, and poor, timid Gretchen received a loaf scarcely half the size of the one she got the first day. When she came home, and her mother cut the loaf open, many new, shining pieces of silver fell out of it.

5. Her mother was very much alarmed, and said, "Take the money back to the good gentleman at once, for it must have got into the dough by accident[5]. Be quick, Gretchen! be quick!"

6. But when the little girl gave the rich man her mother's message[6], he said, "No, no, my child, it was no mistake. I had the silver pieces put into the smallest loaf to reward you. Always be as contented, peaceable[7], and grateful as you now are. Go home now, and tell your mother that the money is your own."

【中文阅读】

1. 从前，发生了一场饥荒。有一位富有的面包师让人叫来了城里最穷苦的 20 个小孩，对他们说："在这个篮子里，你们每个人都可以拿一条面包。拿去吧，以后每天这个时候回到我这里来，直到上帝赐给我们好转的时势为止。"

2. 饥饿的孩子们急忙围拢在篮子周围，他们为了面包互相争吵，因为每个人都希望拿到最大的那条面包。最终，他们连"谢谢"也没对那位善良的先生说一句就走了。

---

1 Gretchen, *a girl's name—the shortened form, or pet name, for Marguerite.*

2 Remained, *staid.*

3 Distance, *place which is far off.*

4 ill-behaved, *rude, having bad manners.*

5 Accident, *mistake.*

6 Message, *word sent, communication.*

7 Peaceable, *quiet, gentle.*

3. 然而，格雷琴，一个衣衫褴褛的小姑娘，并没有和其他人争抢，而是一直谦卑地站在远处。当那些举止失礼的女孩们离去之后，她拿出篮子里仅剩的最小的那条面包，亲吻面包师先生的手，然后回家了。

4. 第二天，那些孩子们和第一天一样没礼貌。而穷苦、羞怯的格雷琴得到了更小的面包，几乎只有前一天那条面包一半大。当她回到家，妈妈把面包条切开的时候，许多崭新的、闪闪发亮的银币掉了出来。

5. 她的妈妈吓呆了，说："马上把这些钱拿回去还给那位仁慈的先生，这些钱肯定是意外掉进面团里的。赶快去，格雷琴，赶快！"

6. 然而，当小姑娘把妈妈说的话告诉那位有钱人的时候，先生说："不，不，我的孩子，那没弄错。我让人把这些银币放进最小的面包条里，是为了奖励你。希望你永远像现在这样，保持知足、平和、感恩的心。现在回家去吧，告诉妈妈，这些钱是你们自己的。"

LESSON 67
SUSIE AND ROVER

◇

苏茜与罗孚

1. "Mamma," said Susie Dean, one summer's morning, "may I go to the woods, and pick berries?"

2. "Yes," replied Mrs. Dean, "but you must take Rover with you."

3. Susie brought her little basket, and her mother put up a nice lunch for her. She tied down the cover, and fastened a tin cup to it.

4. The little girl called Rover—a great Newfoundland dog—and gave him a tin pail to carry. "If I bring it home full, mamma," she said, "won't you make some berry cakes for tea?"

5. Away she tripped, singing as she went down the lane and across the pasture. When she got to the woods, she put her dinner basket down beside a tree, and began to pick berries.

6. Rover ran about, chasing a squirrel or a rabbit now and then, but never straying far from Susie.

7. The tin pail was not a very small one. By the time it was two thirds full, Susie began to feel hungry, and thought she would eat her lunch.

8. Rover came and took his place at her side as soon as she began to eat. Did she not give him some of the lunch? No, she was in a selfish[1] mood[2], and did no such thing.

9. "There, Rover, run away! there's a good dog," she said; but Rover staid near her, watching her steadily[3] with his clear brown eyes.

10. The meat he wanted so much, was soon eaten up; and all he got of the nice dinner, was a small crust of gingerbread that Susie threw away.

---

1 Selfish, *thinking and caring only for one's self.*

2 Mood, *state of mind.*

3 Steadily, *constantly.*

11. After dinner, Susie played a while by the brook. She threw sticks into the water, and Rover swam in and brought them back. Then she began to pick berries again.

12. She did not enjoy the afternoon as she did the morning. The sunshine was as bright, the berries were as sweet and plentiful[1], and she was neither[2] tired nor hungry.

13. But good, faithful Rover was hungry, and she had not given him even one piece of meat. She tried to forget how selfish she had been; but she could not do so, and quite early she started for home.

14. When she was nearly out of the woods, a rustling in the underbrush[3] attracted[4] her attention[5]. "I wonder if that is a bird or a squirrel," said she to herself. "If I can catch it, how glad I shall be!"

---

1 Plentiful, *abundant.*

2 Neither, *not the one or the other.*

3 Underbrush, *shrubs or small bushes in a forest.*

4 Attracted, *drew.*

5 Attention, *earnest thought.*

15. She tried to make her way quietly through the underbrush; but what was her terror[1] when she saw a large snake coiled up before her, prepared for a spring!

16. She was so much frightened that she could not move; but brave Rover saw the snake, and, springing forward, seized it by the neck and killed it.

17. When the faithful dog came and rubbed his head against her hand, Susie put her arms around his neck, and burst into tears. "O Rover," she cried, "you dear, good dog! How sorry I am that I was so selfish!"

18. Rover understood the tone of her voice, if he did not understand her words, and capered[2] about in great glee, barking all the time. You may be sure that he had a plentiful supper that evening.

19. Susie never forgot the lesson of that day. She soon learned to be on her guard against a selfish spirit, and became a happier and more lovable little girl.

(*Mrs. M. O. Johnson*)

【中文阅读】

1. "妈妈，"一个夏日的早晨，苏茜·迪恩说，"我可不可以到树林里去采浆果？"

2. "可以，"迪恩太太回答，"但是你必须带着罗孚一起去。"

3. 苏茜带上她的小篮子，妈妈为她准备了美味的午餐。她把盖子绑紧，再在上面系上一个杯子。

4. 小女孩呼唤罗孚——一条很棒的纽芬兰犬——再给它一个锡桶叼着。"要是我装满这个桶带回家来，妈妈，"她说，"你会不会做一些浆果蛋糕在喝茶的时候吃呢？"

5. 她轻快地走了出去，唱着歌儿，顺着小路，穿过了牧场。到了树林里，她把装着午餐的篮子放在一棵树下，开始采起浆果来。

6. 罗孚跑来跑去，不时追赶松鼠或野兔，但绝对不会离开苏茜太远。

7. 锡桶并不小。到浆果装满了桶的三分之二的时候，苏茜开始觉得饿了，

---

1 Terror, *fright, fear.*

2 Capered, *frisked.*

想起来该吃午饭了。

8. 苏茜开始吃饭时，罗孚马上跑过来，在她身边找个位置蹲好。不给它分一点儿吗？不，苏茜有些自私的情绪，没有给罗孚食物。

9. "罗孚，那边，快走开！乖。"她说。可是罗孚在她身边一动也不动，清澈的褐色眼睛默默地注视着她。

10. 它多想要那块肉啊，可是很快就被吃掉了；这顿美味的午餐它唯一得到的，就是苏茜扔掉的一小块姜饼皮。

11. 吃完以后，苏茜在小河边玩了一会儿。她把棍子扔到水里，罗孚游出去把它叼回来。之后她又开始采浆果了。

12. 下午她并没有像早上那么开心。阳光一样明亮，浆果也一样多而甜美，她并不累，也不饿。

13. 然而又乖又忠诚的罗孚却饿着肚子，她连一小片肉也没有给它。她试图忘掉自己是多么自私，可是却做不到。时间还早，可是她决定提前回家。

14. 当她快要走出树林的时候，灌木丛里传来沙沙作响的声音，引起了她的注意。"我想知道那是只小鸟还是松鼠，"她心里想，"如果我能抓住它，我该多高兴啊！"

15. 她努力让自己不发出任何声音，悄悄爬过灌木丛。当她看见一条大蛇盘踞在她面前的时候，简直吓呆了。那条蛇卷成一圈，随时准备一跃而起！

16. 她害怕得无法动弹。然而勇敢的罗孚一看见这条蛇，就跳上前去，咬住蛇的脖子，把它咬死了。

17. 忠心的小狗跑回来，头在苏茜的手上蹭来蹭去。苏茜双手抱住它的脖子，禁不住大哭起来。"噢，罗孚，"她呼喊着，"亲爱的乖小狗！我好后悔，我那么自私！"

18. 罗孚即便听不懂苏茜说的话，也能理解她的声调和语气。它快乐地跳来跳去，不停地吠叫。你也许猜到了，它那天的晚餐非常丰盛。

19. 苏茜从不忘怀那天的教训。她很快学会了随时警惕自私心理的出现，变成了一个更快乐、更可爱的小女孩。

（M·O·约翰逊夫人）

LESSON 68

THE VIOLET

◇

紫罗兰

1. Down in a green and shady bed,
   A modest violet grew;
   Its stalk was bent, it hung its head,
   As if to hide from view.

2. And yet it was a lovely flower,
   Its colors bright and fair;
   It might have graced a rosy bower
   Instead of hiding there.

3. Yet there it was content to bloom,
   In modest tints arrayed,

And there it spread its sweet perfume,
　　Within the silent shade.

4. Then let me to the valley go,
　　This pretty flower to see;
That I may also learn to grow
　　In sweet humility.

(Jane Taylor)

【中文阅读】

1. 翠绿幽深的谷底，
　生长着谦卑的紫罗兰；
　它弯着腰，把头低，
　似是要躲避人们的视线。

2. 可它的花朵是多么可爱，
　颜色明艳又漂亮；
　她本应在树荫下大放异彩，
　而不是悄然躲藏。

3. 而她安于朴素色调的装扮，
　心甘情愿地开放；
　默默地在阴影里面，
　吐露甜美的芬芳。

4. 那么让我去那山谷里，
　去看看那美丽的紫罗兰花，
　我也能向它学习，
　怀着美好谦逊的心灵长大。

（简·泰勒）

LESSON 69

NO CROWN FOR ME

不要给我花冠

1. "Will you come with us, Susan?" cried several little girls to a schoolmate. "We are going to the woods; do come, too."

2. "I should like to go with you very much," replied Susan, with a sigh; "but I can not finish the task grandmother set me to do."

3. "How tiresome[1] it must be to stay at home to work on a holiday!" said one of the girls, with a toss of her head. "Susan's grandmother is too strict."

4. Susan heard this remark, and, as she bent her head over her task, she wiped away a tear, and thought of the pleasant afternoon the girls would spend gathering wild flowers in the woods.

5. Soon she said to herself, "What harm can there be in moving the mark grandmother put in the stocking? The woods must be very beautiful to-day, and how I should like to be in them!"

6. "Grandmother," said she, a few minutes afterwards, "I am ready, now." "What, so soon, Susan?" Her grandmother took the work, and looked at it very closely.

7. "True, Susan," said she, laying great stress[2] on each word; "true, I count twenty turns from the mark; and, as you have never deceived me, you may go and amuse yourself as you like the rest of the day."

8. Susan's cheeks were scarlet, and she did not say, "Thank you." As she left the cottage, she walked slowly away, not singing as usual.

9. "Why, here is Susan!" the girls cried, when she joined their company[3];

---

1 Tiresome, *tedious, wearisome.*

2 Stress, *force, emphasis.*

3 Company, *a number of persons together.*

"but what is the matter? Why have you left your dear, old grandmother?" they tauntingly[1] added.

10. "There is nothing the matter." As Susan repeated these words, she felt that she was trying to deceive herself. She had acted a lie. At the same time she remembered her grandmother's words, "You have never deceived me."

11. "Yes, I have deceived her," said she to herself. "If she knew all, she would never trust me again."

12. When the little party had reached an open space in the woods, her companions ran about enjoying themselves; but Susan sat on the grass, wishing she were at home confessing[2] her fault[3].

13. After a while Rose cried out, "Let us make a crown of violets, and put it on the head of the best girl here."

---

1 Tauntingly, *in a disagreeable, reproachful manner.*

2 Confessing, *telling of, acknowledging.*

3 Fault, *wrongdoing, sin.*

14. "It will be easy enough to make the crown, but not so easy to decide who is to wear it," said Julia.

15. "Why, Susan is to wear it, of course," said Rose: "is she not said to be the best girl in school and the most obedient at home?"

16. "Yes, yes; the crown shall be for Susan," cried the other girls, and they began to make the crown. It was soon finished.

17. "Now, Susan," said Rose, "put it on in a very dignified[1] way, for you are to be our queen."

18. As these words were spoken, the crown was placed on her head. In a moment she snatched it off, and threw it on the ground, saying, "No crown for me; I do not deserve it."

19. The girls looked at her with surprise. "I have deceived my grandmother," said she, while tears flowed down her cheeks. "I altered[2] the mark she put in the stocking, that I might join you in the woods."

20. "Do you call that wicked?" asked one of the girls.

"I am quite sure it is; and I have been miserable[3] all the time I have been here."

21. Susan now ran home, and as soon as she got there she said, with a beating heart, "O grandmother! I deserve to be punished, for I altered the mark you put in the stocking. Do forgive me; I am very sorry and unhappy."

22. "Susan," said her grandmother, "I knew it all the time; but I let you go out, hoping that your own conscience would tell you of your sin. I am so glad that you have confessed your fault and your sorrow."

23. "When shall I be your own little girl again?" "Now," was the quick reply, and Susan's grandmother kissed her forehead[4].

【中文阅读】

1. "苏珊，你一起来吗？" 几个小女孩向她们的一位同学呼喊，"我们要去

---

1 Dignified, *respectful, stately.*

2 Altered, *changed.*

3 Miserable, *wretched. very unhappy.*

4 Forehead, *the front part of the head above the eyes.*

树林里，你也来吧！"

2. "我很想跟你们一起去，"苏珊叹了一口气，回答道，"可是我还没完成奶奶交给我的任务。"

3. "放假还待在家里干活儿多没劲儿啊！"其中一个女孩晃着脑袋说，"苏珊的奶奶太严厉了。"

4. 苏珊听到了这句评语，当她转身低头继续干活时，拭去了眼中的一滴泪水，想象着女孩们将在树林里采摘野花，度过一个愉快的下午。

5. 很快她对自己说："把奶奶放在袜子里的标志挪用一下又能有什么害处呢？今天树林里一定很美，而我是多么想和她们一起啊！"

6. "奶奶，"过了几分钟之后，她说，"我做好了，就是现在。""什么，苏珊，这么快？"奶奶接过苏珊的作品，仔细查看。

7. "没错，苏珊，"她说，每一个字都咬得很重，"没错，我数过了，标志上有二十个圈；而且，因为你从来没有欺骗过我，今天剩下的时间你可以去做你喜欢做的事情了。"

8. 苏珊的脸颊红了起来，她也没说"谢谢"。在离开小屋的时候，她走得很慢，没有像平常那样唱着歌走开。

9. "咦，苏珊来了！"苏珊加入女孩们的时候，她们高声喊了起来。"可这是怎么回事呢？你为什么离开你亲爱的老奶奶呢？"她们语带讥讽地问。

10. "什么事也没有。"当苏珊重复这句话的时候，她觉得自己是在试图骗自己。她已经撒了一个谎。同时记起了奶奶跟她说的话："你从来没有骗过我。"

11. "我骗了她，"她在心里对自己说，"如果她知道真相，肯定再也不会再信任我了。"

12. 她们的小聚会转移到树林里的一块空地，同伴们跑来跑去非常开心，然而苏珊却坐在草地上，希望自己是在家里，正在承认自己的错误。

13. 过了一会儿，罗斯高声说："我们用紫罗兰编一个花冠吧，把它戴在这里最好的女孩的头上。"

14. "编花冠不难，可是要决定谁可以戴上它就不容易了。"茱莉亚说。

15. "谁说的，当然是苏珊戴上它，"罗斯说，"难道她不是公认在学校里学习最好、在家里最听话的女孩吗？"

16. "对对对，花冠应该属于苏珊。"其他女孩叫道，她们开始编织花冠，很快就编好了。

17. "来，苏珊，"罗斯说，"仪态高贵地把它戴上，因为你是我们的皇后。"

18. 话音刚落，花冠就戴在了苏珊的头上。过了一会儿，她突然把花冠扯了下来，扔在地上，说："不要给我花冠，我不配戴它。"

19. 女孩们惊讶地看着她。"我欺骗了我的奶奶，"苏珊说，泪水顺着她的脸颊流了下来。"我挪用了她放在袜子里的标志，所以我才能到树林里来和你们一起玩。"

20. "你认为这是坏事？"一个女孩问道。

"我很肯定这是坏事，我待在这里一直感到很痛苦。"

21. 此时，苏珊往家的方向飞奔起来。一回到家，心还"怦怦"跳着，"噢，奶奶！我应该受罚，因为我挪用了你放在袜子里的标志。请千万要原谅我，我一直感到歉疚和不开心。"

22. "苏珊，"奶奶开口说，"我从一开始就知道，但我还是让你出去玩，希望你自己的良心会告诉你自己的过错。我很高兴你承认了自己的错误，并且为此感到伤心。"

23. "我什么时候可以变回你亲爱的小孙女呢？""现在！"回答很迅速。奶奶在苏珊的前额印上一个吻。

LESSON 70
YOUNG SOLDIERS

◇

小战士

1. Oh, were you ne'er a schoolboy,
    And did you never train,
   And feel that swelling of the heart
    You ne'er can feel again?

2. Did you never meet, far down the street,
    With plumes and banners gay,
   While the kettle, for the kettledrum[1],
    Played your march, march away?

1 Kettledrum, *a drum made of a copper vessel shaped like a kettle.*

3. It seems to me but yesterday,
   Nor scarce so long ago,
   Since all our school their muskets[1] took,
   To charge the fearful foe.

4. Our muskets were of cedar[2] wood,
   With ramrods bright and new;
   With bayonets[3] forever set,
   And painted barrels[4], too.

5. We charged upon a flock of geese,
   And put them all to flight—
   Except one sturdy[5] gander
   That thought to show us fight.

6. But, ah! we knew a thing or two;
   Our captain wheeled the van[6];
   We routed[7] him, we scouted[8] him,
   Nor lost a single man!

7. Our captain was as brave a lad
   As e'er commission[9] bore;
   And brightly shone his new tin sword;
   A paper cap he wore.

8. He led us up the steep hillside,
   Against the western wind,

---

1 Muskets, *a kind of gun.*
2 Cedar, *a very durable kind of wood.*
3 Bayonets, *a sharp piece of steel on the end of a gun.*
4 Barrels, *the long metal tube forming part of a gun.*
5 Sturdy, *stubborn, bold.*
6 Van, *the front.*
7 Routed, *put to flight.*
8 Scouted, *made fun of.*
9 Commission, *a writing to show power.*

While the cockerel[1] plume that decked his head
Streamed bravely out behind.

9. We shouldered arms, we carried arms,
   We charged[2] the bayonet;
   And woe unto the mullein[3] stalk
   That in our course we met!

10. At two o'clock the roll we called,
    And till the close of day,
    With fearless hearts, though tired limbs,
    We fought the mimic fray[4],—
    Till the supper bell, from out the dell,
    Bade us march, march away.

【中文阅读】

1. 噢，还记得你曾是个小男生吗？
   还记得你曾日夜操练，
   感到血脉贲张满怀豪情，
   那种感觉如今已消失不见？

---

1 Cockerel, *a young chicken-cock.*

2 Charged, *made an onset.*

3 Mullein, *a tall plant that grows in neglected fields.*

4 Fray, *fight, contest.*

2. 难道你不曾在街边上，
   遇上挥舞鲜艳羽毛和旗帜的队伍，
   当作鼓的水壶咚咚敲着进行曲，
   伴随你行进的每一步？

3. 似乎就在不久以前，
   对我来说一切恍如昨日，
   我们全都举着步枪，
   向着可怕的敌人冲刺。

4. 那杉木做的步枪，
   带有簇新的推弹杆；
   刺刀固定在枪上，
   还有上了漆的枪管。

5. 我们向一群鹅发起攻击，
   吓得它们四处飞散。
   除了一只强壮的雄鹅，
   想要和我们决一死战。

6. 可是，啊！我们可精于此道，
   我们的首领冲在前面；
   我们打得它落荒而逃，大肆嘲笑，
   而我军一个人都没不见！

7. 我们的队长是个勇敢的小伙子，
   就像委任状上写的那样；
   他头戴纸帽，
   亮出新的铁剑闪闪发光。

8. 他带领我们爬上陡峭的山坡，
   猎猎西风迎面而来，
   他头上插着的公鸡羽毛，
   迎风飘扬的样子多么豪迈。

9. 我们扛枪上肩，我们全副武装，
   我们把刺刀都装上；
   毛蕊花茎不幸遭了殃，
   谁叫它挡在我们奔跑的路上！

10. 两点钟我们就点名集合，
    一直玩到夜幕降临，
    我们投入模拟的战斗，
    心无所畏惧，手脚却筋疲力尽，
    直到树林外面传来晚饭的呼唤，
    迫使我们踏步走出树林。

LESSON 71

HOW WILLIE GOT OUT OF THE SHAFT

❖

威利是怎样逃出枯井的

1. Willie's aunt sent him for a birthday[1] present a little writing book. There was a place in the book for a pencil. Willie thought a great deal of this little book, and always kept it in his pocket.

2. One day, his mother was very busy, and he called his dog, and said, "Come, Caper, let us have a play."

---

1 Birthday, *the same day of the month in which a person was born, in each succeeding year.*

3. When Willie's mother missed him, she went to the door and looked out, and could not see him anywhere; but she knew that Caper was with him, and thought they would come back before long.

4. She waited an hour, and still they did not come. When she came to the gate by the road, she met Mr. Lee, and told him how long Willie had been gone. Mr. Lee thought he must have gone to sleep under the trees. So they went to all the trees under which Willie was in the habit of playing, but he was nowhere to be found.

5. By this time the sun had gone down. The news that Willie was lost soon spread over the neighborhood[1], and all the men and women[2] turned out to hunt. They hunted all night.

6. The next morning the neighbors were gathered round, and all were trying to think what to do next, when Caper came bounding into the room. There was a string tied round his neck, and a bit of paper tied to it.

7. Willie's father, Mr. Lee, took the paper, and saw that it was a letter from Willie. He read it aloud. It said, "O father! come to me. I am in the big hole in the pasture."

8. Everybody ran at once to the far corner of the pasture; and there was Willie, alive and well, in the shaft[3]. Oh, how glad he was when his father caught him in his arms, and lifted him out!

9. Now I will tell you how Willie came to be in the shaft. He and Caper went to the pasture field, and came to the edge of the shaft and sat down. In bending over to see how deep it was, he lost his balance, and fell in. He tried very hard to get out, but could not.

10. When the good little dog saw that his master was in the shaft, he would not leave him, but ran round and round, reaching down and trying to pull him out. But while Caper was pulling Willie by the coat sleeves, a piece of sod gave way under his feet, and he fell in too.

11. Willie called for his father and mother as loud as he could call; but he was so far away from the house that no one could hear him.

12. He cried and called till it was dark, and then he lay down on the

---

1 Neighborhood, *the surrounding region which lies nearest, vicinity.*

2 Women, *plural of woman.*

3 Shaft, *a deep hole made in the earth, usually for mining purposes.*

224

ground, and Caper lay down close beside him. It was not long before Willie cried himself to sleep.

13. When he awoke it was morning, and he began to think of a way to get out. The little writing book that his aunt had given him, was in his pocket. He took it out, and, after a good deal of trouble, wrote the letter to his father.

14. Then he tore the leaf out, and took a string out of his pocket, and tied it round Caper's neck, and tied the letter to the string. Then he lifted the dog up, and helped him out, and said to him, "Go home, Caper, go home!" The little dog scampered[1] away, and was soon at home.

【中文阅读】

1. 威利的阿姨送了他一个笔记本作为生日礼物。本子上有个地方插着铅笔。威利非常喜欢这个小本子，总是把它放在口袋里。

2. 有一天，威利的妈妈很忙。威利把他的小狗叫过来："凯普过来，咱们玩个游戏。"

3. 当威利的妈妈想起他来，她走到门口四处张望，却哪儿也没有威利的身影。妈妈知道小狗凯普和威利在一起，心想他们不久之后自然就会回来。

4. 等了一个小时，他们还是没有回来。她走到路边的大门口，遇到了李先生，于是告诉他威利有多久不见踪影了。李先生猜想威利一定是在树荫下睡着了。于是他们到威利平常习惯去玩耍的地方寻找，然而所有的树底下，都没有找到小威利。

5. 到了太阳下山的时候，"威利不见了"的消息已经迅速传开。邻居们男男女女都到外面帮忙寻找，足足找了一整夜。

6. 第二天早晨，邻居们聚集在房间里。大家都一筹莫展，想不出下一步应该怎么做。就在这个时候，小狗凯普突然跑了进来。在凯普的脖子上系着一根绳子，绑着一张小纸条。

7. 威利的爸爸李先生取下了纸条，发现那是威利写的一封信。他大声地读出来，信上是这样写的："噢，爸爸！快来救我！我在牧场的那个大坑里。"

---

1 Scampered, *ran briskly.*

8. 所有人马上跑到牧场那个遥远的角落，威利果然在那个枯井里，安然无恙。噢，当父亲的双臂抱起威利，把他拉到井外的那一刻，威利多么高兴啊！

9. 好了，现在我来告诉你威利是怎么掉进枯井里去的。他和凯普到牧场上玩耍，来到枯井的边缘坐了下来。在弯腰看井有多深的时候，威利失去平衡掉了下去。他做了很大的努力，却怎么也爬不上来。

10. 小狗看见主人掉进了井里，它始终不离不弃，绕着井口跑来跑去，还往下探身子试图把他拉上来。可是就在凯普咬着威利外套的袖子往上拉的时候，它脚下的一块草皮松了，于是凯普也滑进了井里。

11. 威利用尽最大的声音使劲喊爸爸妈妈，然而他离家太远了，根本没有人听见他的呼喊。

12. 他又哭又喊直到天黑，然后躺倒在地上，凯普也在他身边躺了下来。威利哭着哭着，没多久就睡着了。

13. 到威利醒过来的时候已经天亮了，他开始想办法离开这个地方。他想起了口袋里阿姨送给他小本子。威利把小本子掏了出来，费了半天的劲儿，写了那封给爸爸的信。

14. 写完之后，威利撕下了那一页纸，从口袋里拿出一根绳子，绑在凯普的脖子上，再把信绑紧。然后，他把小狗举起来，帮助它爬了上去，对它说："回家，凯普，回家！"小狗马上飞奔起来，很快就到家了。

LESSON 72
THE PERT CHICKEN

◆

无礼的小公鸡

1. There was once a pretty chicken;
    But his friends were very few,
For he thought that there was nothing
    In the world but what he knew:
So he always, in the farmyard[1],
    Had a very forward[2] way,

---

1 Farmyard, *the inclosed ground attached to a barn and other farm buildings.*
2 Forward, *bold, confident.*

Telling all the hens and turkeys[1]
　　What they ought to do and say.
"Mrs. Goose," he said, "I wonder
　　That your goslings[2] you should let
Go out paddling[3] in the water;
　　It will kill them to get wet."

2. "I wish, my old Aunt Dorking[4],"
　　He began to her, one day,
"That you wouldn't sit all summer
　　In your nest upon the hay.
Won't you come out to the meadow,
　　Where the grass with seeds is filled?"
"If I should," said Mrs. Dorking,
　　"Then my eggs would all get chilled."
"No, they won't," replied the chicken,
　　"And no matter if they do;
Eggs are really good for nothing;
　　What's an egg to me or you?"

3. "What's an egg!" said Mrs. Dorking,
　　"Can it be you do not know
You yourself were in an eggshell
　　Just one little month ago?
And, if kind wings had not warmed you,
　　You would not be out to-day,
Telling hens, and geese, and turkeys,
　　What they ought to do and say!

4. "To be very wise, and show it,

1　Turkeys, *a large domestic fowl.*
2　Goslings, *young geese.*
3　Paddling, *beating the water with the feet, swimming.*
4　Dorking, *a species of chicken.*

228

Is a pleasant thing, no doubt;
But, when young folks talk to old folks,
They should know what they're about."

(Marian Douglas)

【中文阅读】

1. 从前有只漂亮的小公鸡，
   他的朋友却没几个；
   因为他认为这个世界上
   没有什么是他不知道的；
   所以在农家小院里，
   总看见他直冲向前大言不惭
   告诉所有母鸡和火鸡，
   什么该说，什么该干。
   他说："鹅太太，我想你太不应该，
   让小鹅们到外面玩耍；
   他们在水里扑腾嬉戏，
   全身湿透随时会没命的呀。"

2. 有一天，他又对道根鸡开口：
   "我希望，我亲爱的道根鸡阿姨，
   你不要整个夏天都坐着不动，
   老在干草上蹲窝有什么意思！
   难道你就不想在草地上走走？
   那里多的是种子藏在草里。"
   "如果我走开，"道根鸡阿姨回答他，
   "那我的蛋全都会冻死。"
   "不，它们不会的，"小公鸡接话，

"就算它们冻坏也没问题。
那些蛋一点好处也没有，
对你对我又有什么意义？"

3."蛋有什么意义！"道根鸡大声说，
"它可以是你不知道的一切。
你可知短短一个月之前的自己，
还在蛋壳里没来到这个世界？
如果不是有慈爱的翅膀给你温暖，
今天你就不会在这里出现，
对着母鸡、火鸡和鹅妈妈，
说它们什么该说，什么该干！"

4."做个聪明人到处炫耀，
毫无疑问你会感觉愉快；
可是当年轻人面对长者说话，
最好他们说的东西要自己先明白。"

（玛丽安·道格拉斯）

LESSON 73
INDIAN CORN

— ◇ —

印第安玉米

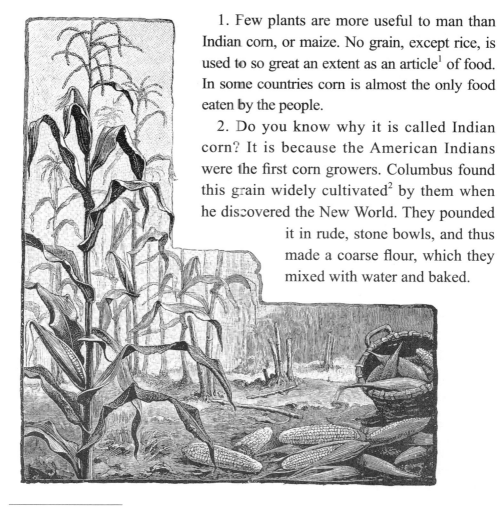

1. Few plants are more useful to man than Indian corn, or maize. No grain, except rice, is used to so great an extent as an article[1] of food. In some countries corn is almost the only food eaten by the people.

2. Do you know why it is called Indian corn? It is because the American Indians were the first corn growers. Columbus found this grain widely cultivated[2] by them when he discovered the New World. They pounded it in rude, stone bowls, and thus made a coarse flour, which they mixed with water and baked.

---

1 Article, *a particular one of various things.*
2 Cultivated, *grown.*

3. Indian corn is now the leading crop in the United States. In whatever part of this land we live, we see corn growing every year in its proper season. Yet how few can tell the most simple and important[1] facts about its planting and its growth!

4. Corn, to do well, must have a rich soil and a warm climate. It is a tender plant, and is easily injured by cold weather. The seed corn does not sprout, but rots, if the ground is cold and wet.

5. To prepare land properly for planting corn, the soil is made fine by plowing, and furrows[2] are run across the field four feet apart each way. At every point where these furrows cross, the farmer drops from four to seven grains of seed corn. These are then covered with about two inches of earth, and thus form "hills" of corn.

6. In favorable[3] weather, the tender blades push through the ground in ten days or two weeks; then the stalks mount up rapidly, and the long, streamer[4]-like leaves unfold gracefully from day to day. Corn must be carefully cultivated while the plants are small. After they begin to shade the ground, they need but little hoeing or plowing.

7. The moisture[5] and earthy matter, drawn through the roots, become sap. This passes through the stalk, and enters the leaves. There a great change takes place which results[6] in the starting of the ears and the growth of the grain.

8. The maize plant bears two kinds of flowers,—male and female. The two are widely separated[7]. The male flowers are on the tassel; the fine silk threads which surround the ear, and peep out from the end of the husks, are the female flowers.

9. Each grain on the cob is the starting point for a thread of silk; and, unless the thread receives some particle[8] of the dust which falls from the tassel flowers, the kernel with which it is connected will not grow.

---

1 Important, *of much value.*
2 Furrows, *a trench made by a plow.*
3 Favorable, *that which is kindly, propitious.*
4 Streamer, *a long, narrow flag.*
5 Moisture, *wet, dampness.*
6 Results, *comes out, ends.*
7 Separated, *apart, not connected.*
8 Particle, *a very small portion.*

10. The many uses of Indian corn and its products are worthy of note. The green stalks and leaves make excellent[1] fodder[2] for cattle. The ripe grain is used all over the earth as food for horses, pigs, and poultry[3]. Nothing is better for fattening stock.

11. Green corn, or "roasting ears," hulled corn and hominy, New England hasty pudding, and succotash[4] are favorite dishes with many persons. Then there are parched corn and pop corn—the delight of long winter evenings.

12. Cornstarch is an important article of commerce[5]. Sirup and sugar are made from the juice of the stalk, and oil and alcohol[6] from the ripened grain. Corn husks are largely used for filling mattresses[7], and are braided[8] into mats, baskets, and other useful articles.

13. Thus it will be seen how varied are the uses of Indian corn. And besides being so useful, the plant is very beautiful. The sight of a large cornfield in the latter part of summer, with all its green banners waving and its tasseled plumes nodding, is one to admire, and not to be forgotten.

【中文阅读】

1. 很少有别的植物像印第安玉米（也叫玉蜀黍）那么有用。除了大米以外，没有哪一种农作物像玉米一样被如此广泛地用作粮食。在某些国家，玉米几乎是人们唯一的食粮。

2. 你知道印第安玉米这个称呼是怎么来的吗？那是因为美洲的印第安人是最早种植玉米的人。哥伦布发现新大陆的时候，也发现了印第安人大面积地种植这种农作物。他们把玉米放在粗糙的石碗里捣碎，做成粗粝的玉米面，和上水就可以烘烤成玉米饼了。

3. 印第安玉米是美国目前最主要的农作物。在我们生活的这片土地上，无

---

1 Excellent, *good, superior.*

2 Fodder, *such food for animals as hay, straw, and vegetables.*

3 Poultry, *barnyard fowls.*

4 Succotash, *corn and beans boiled together.*

5 Commerce, *trade.*

6 Alcohol, *distilled liquor.*

7 Mattresses, *beds stuffed with hair, straw, or other soft material.*

8 Braided, *woven or twisted together.*

论哪个地区，每年在相应的季节，我们都可以看到玉米苗壮生长。然而，尽管并不复杂，又有多少人能够说出这种作物是如何种植和生长的呢！

4. 要让玉米生长得好，必须要有肥沃的土壤和温暖的气候。这种柔弱的植物很容易被寒冷天气摧毁。如果土地变得又冷又湿，玉米的种子就不会发芽，而会腐烂。

5. 为种植玉米而准备的土地，必须通过翻耕使土壤适于种植，一块地分成许多小块，任一方向每 4 英尺以土沟分隔。在土沟纵横交叉之处，农夫撒下 4~7 粒玉米种子，埋在大约两英寸的土壤之下，这样就形成了"玉米堆"。

6. 只要天气适宜，十天到两周之后，柔弱的种子就会扎根在土壤里，很快枝茎破土而出，越长越高。一天一天过去，丝带一样的叶子也优雅地舒展开来。在玉米还是幼苗的时候，必须细心照料。然而当它们长高，盖住了土地之后，就几乎不再需要耕作了。

7. 玉米的根从土壤里吸取水分和养分，成为树液，经由茎部传输到叶子。这为植物带来巨大的变化，因此得以抽穗，最终长出颗粒。

8. 玉米开的花有两种——雄花和雌花。两种花很不一样，雄花呈穗状；而那种围绕着包谷生长并在包皮的末端隐约露出的丝一样的细线，就是雌花。

9. 玉米穗轴上的每一个颗粒都是一束丝状雌花的起点，除非花束获得来自于穗状雄花的微粒，否则它所连接的内核就无法成长。

10. 印第安玉米及其产品的广泛用途值得详细注解：绿色的玉米茎和叶子是喂牛的好饲料。成熟的玉米粒在全世界都被广泛用作饲料，喂养马、猪、家禽等。它还是最好的积肥用料。

11. 嫩玉米、烤或煮熟的玉米、去皮玉米、玉米粥、新英格兰玉米粉糊或是豆煮玉米是许多人们的最爱。还有烘烤玉米片和爆米花，在漫漫冬夜里为人们带来欢乐。

12. 玉米淀粉是一种重要的商品。玉米茎的汁液是提炼糖和糖浆的原料。成熟的玉米粒是油和酒精的来源。玉米的包皮用途也很广泛，它可以是床垫的填充物，或者经过编织成为各种垫子、篮子和其他用品。

13. 由此可见，印第安玉米全身都是宝。它不但用途多样，还是一种美丽的植物。盛夏时节，一望无际的玉米地，绿色的叶子像旗帜一样迎风飞舞，流苏璎珞般的包谷随风点头，这是多么赏心悦目而又令人难忘的景色！

LESSON 74
THE SNOWBIRD'S SONG

◇

雪鸟之歌

1. The ground was all covered with snow one day,
   And two little sisters were busy at play,
   When a snowbird was sitting close by on a tree,
   And merrily singing his chick-a-de-dee[1].

---

1 Chick-a-de-dee, *an imitation of the notes of the snowbird.*

2. He had not been singing that tune very long
    Ere Emily heard him, so loud was his song;
  "O sister, look out of the window!" said she;
    "Here's a dear little bird singing chick-a-de-dee.

3. "Poor fellow! he walks in the snow and the sleet,
    And has neither stockings nor shoes on his feet:
  I wonder what makes him so full of his glee;
    He's all the time singing his chick-a-de-dee.

4. "If I were a barefooted snowbird, I know,
    I would not stay out in the cold and the snow;
  I pity him so! oh, how cold he must be!
    And yet he keeps singing his chick-a-de-dee.

5. "O mother; do get him some stockings, and shoes,
    And a nice little frock, and a hat if he choose:
  I wish he'd come into the parlor, and see
    How warm we would make him, poor chick-a-de-dee!"

6. The bird had flown down for some sweet crumbs of bread,
    And heard every word little Emily said:
  "What a figure[1] I'd make in that dress" thought he,
    And laughed as he warbled his chick-a-de-dee.

7. "I am grateful," said he, "for the wish you express[2],
    But have no occasion for such a fine dress;
  I rather remain with my little limbs free,
    Than to hobble[3] about, singing chick-a-de-dee.

8. "There is One, my dear child, though I can not tell who,

---

1 Figure, *shape, appearance.*
2 Express, *make known, declare.*
3 Hobble, *to walk with a hitch or hop.*

Has clothed me already, and warm enough, too.
Good morning! Oh, who are so happy as we?"
And away he flew, singing his chick-a-de-dee.

(F. C. Woodworth)

【中文阅读】

1. 有一天白雪覆盖了大地，
两个小姐妹正玩得忘乎所以；
这时候一只雪鸟停在旁边的树上，
嘀呖呖嘀呖呖愉快地歌唱。

2. 他的音调并不太长，
被艾米丽听到之前，他正高声歌唱；
她说"噢，姐姐，你看看窗外的树上！
有只可爱的小鸟嘀呖呖嘀呖呖在欢唱。"

3. "可怜的小家伙！他走在雨雪里，
脚上没有袜子也没有鞋子；
我想知道是什么让他充满欢乐，
总是嘀呖呖嘀呖呖不停唱着歌。"

4. "我知道，如果我是雪鸟光着脚丫，
我才不会待在寒冷的雪地里任风吹雨打；

我多么同情他！噢，他一定冷得不行！
可是他仍然嘀呖呖嘀呖呖地唱个不停。"

5. "噢，妈妈，请给他穿上鞋袜和袍子，
如果他愿意再让他挑一顶帽子；
我希望他能来到我们的会客室，
看看我们可以让他感到多么温暖，可怜的嘀呖呖！"

6. 雪鸟飞下来去啄地上的甜面包渣，
他听见了艾米丽说的每一句话；
他想："要是我穿上那条裙子会是什么样子？"
他一边笑一边轻声唱着他的嘀呖呖。

7. "我很感激，"他说，"谢谢你们的好意，
但是那么漂亮的裙子对于我实在不合时宜；
我宁愿光着我的脚丫自由自在，
胜过唱着嘀呖呖却一瘸一拐。"

8. "亲爱的小孩，曾经有一个人，虽然我不能说是谁，
曾经给我穿上过衣服既暖和又美；
早上好！噢，谁有我们这么快乐？"
他飞走了，唱着他那嘀呖呖的歌。

（F·C·德沃斯）

LESSON 75

MOUNTAINS

◆

高　山

1. The Himalayas[1] are the highest mountains on our globe, They are in Asia, and separate India from Thibet. They extend in a continuous line for more than a thousand miles.

2. If you ever ascend[2] one of these mountains from the plain below, you will have to cross an unhealthy border, twenty miles in width. It is, in fact,

---

1 Himalayas, *also written Himmaleh.*

2 Ascend, *go up, climb.*

a swamp[1] caused by the waters overflowing the river banks.

3. The soil of this swampy border is covered with trees and shrubs, where the tiger, the elephant, and other animals find secure retreat[2]. Beyond this border, you will reach smiling valleys and noble forests.

4. As you advance[3] onward and upward, you will get among bolder and more rugged[4] scenes. The sides of the mountains are very steep, sometimes well wooded to quite a height, but sometimes quite barren[5].

5. In crossing a river you must be content with three ropes for a bridge. You will find the streets of the towns to be simply stairs cut out of the rock, and see the houses rising in tiers[6].

6. The pathways into Thibet, among these mountains, are mere tracks by the side of foaming torrents. Often, as you advance, you will find every trace of the path swept away by the falling of rocks and earth from above.

7. Sometimes you will find posts driven into the mountain side, upon which branches of trees and earth are spread. This forms a trembling foothold[7] for the traveler.

8. In the Andes[8], in South America, the sure-footed mule is used to carry travelers. Quite often a chasm[9] must be crossed that is many feet wide and hundreds of feet deep. The mule will leap across this chasm, but not until it is sure it can make a safe jump.

9. "One day," says a traveler, "I went by the worst pass over the Andes Mountains. The path for seventy yards was very narrow, and at one point it was washed entirely away. On one side the rock brushed my shoulder, and on the other side my foot overhung the precipice[10]."

10. The guide told this man, after he was safely over the pass, that, to

---

1 Swamp, *low, wet ground.*

2 Retreat, *place of safety.*

3 Advance, *go forward.*

4 Rugged, *rough.*

5 Barren, *without trees or shrubs, unproductive.*

6 Tiers, *rows one above another.*

7 Foothold, *that on which one may tread.*

8 Andes, *next to the highest range of mountains in the world.*

9 Chasm, *a deep opening in the earth, or cleft in the rocks.*

10 Precipice, *a very steep and dangerous descent.*

his knowledge[1], four hundred mules had fallen over that precipice, and in many instances travelers had lost their lives at that terrible spot.

【中文阅读】

1. 喜马拉雅山是地球上最高的山，位于亚洲，在印度与中国西藏之间，山脉连绵超过一千英里。

2. 如果你试图从山脚的平原登上其中一座山峰，你就必须跨越一条危及生命健康的边界线，宽度达到了 20 英里。实际上，那是一片由于河水溢出河床流到岸边形成的沼泽地。

3. 沼泽地的土壤被树林与灌木丛所覆盖，那里是老虎、大象等动物寻找安全退路的所在。跨越了这片边界地，你就能到达开阔的山谷和郁郁葱葱的森林。

4. 当你继续向上攀登，你会置身于更粗糙、更崎岖的山野之间。山崖十分陡峭，有时即便很高的地方也生长着树木，有时则相当贫瘠荒凉。

5. 越过河流的时候，有一条三根绳子做成的桥你就该感到满足了。走进市镇，你会发现街道是直接在岩石上开凿而成，房子一排排拔地而起。

6. 进入西藏的小路蜿蜒在山间，小路一侧就是怒吼着的滚滚洪流，你会发现路上没有任何足迹，因为都被从山上滚落的石头和沙泥一扫而空了。

7. 有时你会看到山崖上插着柱子，在上面铺上树枝和泥土，就形成了让人心惊胆战的立足之地，供旅人通过。

8. 在位于南美洲的安第斯山脉，旅客们使用步伐稳健的骡子作为坐骑。常常在必须跨越好几英尺宽、几百英尺深的峡谷时，这种骡子会一跃而过，当然，如果它们不确定自己可以越过的话，是不会冒险的。

9. "有一天，"一位旅客说，"我遇到了安第斯山脉最糟糕的路况。有一段路长达 70 码，非常狭窄，有一个地方路完全被冲走了。我只好任由一侧的肩膀被岩石摩擦着，另一侧的脚就吊挂在悬崖边上。"

10. 在这位旅客安全通过了那条路之后，一位向导告诉他，据他的了解，在那个悬崖大概摔死过 400 头骡子，还有很多人在那个可怕的地方失去了生命。

---

1 Knowledge, that which is known.

LESSON 76
A CHILD'S HYMN

◇

儿童赞美诗

1. God make my life a little light,
     Within the world to glow;
   A little flame that burneth bright
     Wherever I may go.

2. God make my life a little flower,
     That giveth joy to all,
   Content to bloom in native bower,
     Although its place be small.

3. God make my life a little song,
     That comforteth the sad;
   That helpeth others to be strong,
     And makes the singer glad.

4. God make my life a little hymn
     Of tenderness and praise;
   Of faith—that never waxeth dim
     In all His wondrous ways.

【中文阅读】

1. 上帝把我的生命变成一点光，
　　在这世界发亮；
　　一点星火把光明燃亮，
　　无论我去向何方。

2. 上帝把我的生命变成一朵小花，
　　带给人们欢乐；
　　尽管在小小的角落里生长开花，
　　也在树荫下怡然自得。

3. 上帝把我的生命变成一首小曲，
　　让伤心的人得到安慰；
　　帮助他人更加坚强无惧，
　　唱歌的人也忘掉伤悲。

4. 上帝把我的生命变成一首赞美诗，
　　温柔慈爱，至诚礼赞；
　　虔诚信仰——以一切神奇的方式，
　　永不笼罩阴霾黑暗。

LESSON 77

HOLDING THE FORT

◇

守住堡垒

1. While Genie was walking slowly down street one day, she heard an odd rapping on the pavement[1] behind her. Looking round, she saw Rob Grey hobbling on crutches[2].

2. "Why, what is the matter?" cried Genie. "I haven't seen you for a week, and now you are walking in that way."

3. "I shall have to walk in this way as much as a week longer, Genie. I sprained[3] my ankle by stopping too quick—no, not too quick, either, for

---

1 Pavement, *a walk covered with brick or other hard material.*
2 Crutches, *long sticks with crosspieces at the top, to aid lame persons in walking.*
3 Sprained, *injured by wrenching or twisting.*

244

there was something in my way."

"What was it?" asked Genie.

4. "One of the Commandments[1]," replied Rob. "You remember how that lecturer[2] talked to us about 'holding the fort'? Well, I thought I should like to do it; but it's a pretty long war, you know—all a lifetime, and no vacations[3]—furloughs[4], I think they call them."

5. "If there was nothing to fight, we should not need to be soldiers," said Genie.

6. "Well, I thought I would try; but the first day, when we came out of the schoolhouse, Jack Lee snatched my books out of my hand, and threw them into the mud.

7. "I started after him as fast as I could run. I meant to throw him where he had thrown the books, when, all of a sudden, I thought of the Commandment about returning good for evil.

8. "I stopped short—so short, that, somehow, my foot twisted under me. So, you see, it was one of the commandments."

9. "If one must stumble at them, it is a good thing to fall on the right side," said Genie, with a wise nod of her head.

10. "The whole thing puzzles me, and makes me feel—well, like giving it up," said Rob. "It might have served me right when I was chasing Jack; but when I thought of the Commandment, I really tried to do the right thing."

11. "You did do it, Rob," said Genie. "You 'held the fort' that time. Why, don't you see—you are only a wounded[5] soldier."

12. "I never thought of that," said Rob. "If I believe that way—" He began to whistle, and limped off to school without finishing the sentence. But Genie knew, by the way he behaved[6] that day, that he had made up his mind to *hold the fort.*

---

1 Commandments, *holy laws recorded in the Bible.*

2 Lecturer, *a public speaker.*

3 Vacations, *the time between two school terms.*

4 Furloughs, *a soldier's leave of absense*

5 Wounded, *hurt, injured*

6 Behaved, *acted.*

【中文阅读】

1. 有一天，吉妮在街上慢慢走着，忽然听到后面人行道上传来奇怪的敲击声。回头一看，原来是罗伯·格雷拄着拐杖一瘸一拐地走过来。

2. "怎么了？发生了什么事？"吉妮不禁失声喊道。"一个星期没见你，你走路怎么这个样子？"

3. "接下来至少一个星期我都得这样走路，吉妮。我太快停下来，所以摔坏了膝盖。不，也不是因为停得太快，是因为有东西挡了我的路。"

4. "就是其中一条戒律，"罗伯继续说，"你记得老师跟我们讲过的'守住堡垒'那条戒律吗？啊，我那时想我应该这么做；可是你知道，这是一场持久战——整整一生，没有假期——暂时的休息都不行，我想他们是这么说的。"

5. "如果没有什么需要我们为之战斗，那么我们就不需要成为战士了。"吉妮说。

6. "嗯，我想我会试着去做；但是我们离开校舍的第一天，杰克·李忽然把我手里的书抢了过去，丢在烂泥地里。"

7. "我马上跑去追他，满脑子想着要抓到他，把他推到扔我书的那块烂泥地里。可是忽然间，我想起了'以德报怨'那条戒律。"

8. "我突然停住脚步——那么突然，不知道为什么就把脚给扭了。所以，你看，就是一条戒律把我绊倒的。"

9. "如果一个人必须被戒律绊倒，那么倒向正确的一边也是一件好事。"吉妮一边说，一边睿智地点头。

10. "这件事情让我困惑，使我想要，嗯，想要放弃，"罗伯说，"如果是在我追杰克的时候摔倒，我能想得通，可是当我想起戒律的时候，我是真想做正确的事情啊。"

11. "罗伯，你确实做了正确的事情，"吉妮说，"那一刻你守住了堡垒。怎么，你还不明白吗——只不过你是一名负伤的战士。"

12. "我从来没这么想过，"罗伯说，"要是我这么想的话……"他吹起了口哨，抬起脚一瘸一拐地往学校走去，话也没说完。但是吉妮明白，从罗伯那天的举动就知道，他已经下定决心，要"守住城堡"。

LESSON 78

THE LITTLE PEOPLE

———◇———

小人儿

1. A dreary[1] place would be this earth,
   Were there no little people in it;
   The song of life would lose its mirth,
   Were there no children to begin it;

2. No little forms, like buds to grow,
   And make the admiring heart surrender[2];
   No little hands on breast and brow,
   To keep the thrilling love chords[3] tender.

3. The sterner souls would grow more stern[4],
   Unfeeling nature more inhuman,
   And man to utter[5] coldness turn,
   And woman would be less than woman.

4. Life's song, indeed, would lose its charm,
   Were there no babies to begin it;
   A doleful[6] place this world would be,
   Were there no little people in it.

(John G. Whittier)

---

1 Dreary, *cheerless.*
2 Surrender, *give up, yield.*
3 Chords, *ties of affection.*
4 Stern, *severe, harsh.*
5 Utter, *complete.*
6 Doleful, *gloomy, sad.*

1. 如果没有了小人儿在地球上，
　　这个地方将是多么沉闷无聊；
　　没有了孩子们领头唱，
　　生命之歌将失去欢乐的曲调。

2. 没有了那些小东西，像嫩芽初露，
　　让爱慕的心为之震颤；
　　没有了轻抚于胸前和眉间的小手，
　　让爱的和弦轻柔地奏响于心间。

3. 无情的灵魂只会更无情，
　　麻木的心灵会更残忍，
　　男人现出冷酷言行，
　　女人也不像女人。

4. 确实，如果没有婴儿的初啼，
　　生命之歌将会失去魅力；
　　如果没有了小人儿在这里，
　　世界将会变成寂寞阴沉之地。

（约翰·G·惠蒂尔）

LESSON 79

GOOD NIGHT

◇

晚　安

1. The sun is hidden from our sight,
   The birds are sleeping sound;
   'T is time to say to all, "Good night!"
   And give a kiss all round.

2. Good night, my father, mother, dear!
   Now kiss your little son;
   Good night, my friends, both far and near!
   Good night to every one.

3. Good night, ye merry, merry birds!
   Sleep well till morning light;
   Perhaps, if you could sing in words,
   You would have said, "Good night!"

4. To all my pretty flowers, good night!
   You blossom while I sleep;
   And all the stars, that shine so bright,
   With you their watches keep.

5. The moon is lighting up the skies,
   The stars are sparkling there;
   'T is time to shut our weary eyes,
   And say our evening prayer.

(Mrs. Follen)

1. 太阳藏得我们看不见了，
   鸟儿也静静安眠；
   是时候对大家说"晚安！"
   亲吻每个人的笑脸。

2. 晚安，亲爱的爸爸妈妈！
   请吻吻你们的孩子；
   晚安，我的朋友，无论你是远是近！
   说一句晚安送给你。

3. 晚安，快乐的小鸟！
   睡个好觉直到天亮；
   也许，如果你有歌词配上曲调，
   "晚安！"你唱的肯定也是这样。

4. 我美丽的花儿，晚安！
   你们在我睡着的时候盛开；
   天上所有的星星亮闪闪，
   是要守候你们直到早晨到来。

5. 月儿照亮天边，
   星星闪耀光芒；
   是时候闭上我们疲倦的双眼，
   祈祷之后进入梦乡。

（佛伦夫人）